Table of Contents

CHAPTER 5: TASTY RECIPES

CHAPTER 6: EASY RECIPES

CHAPTER 7: CHAPTER 10: MEDIUM RECIPES

CHAPTER 8: CHAPTER 12: ADVANCED RECIPES

CONCLUSION

Introduction and Education to Dehydration

When you think of dehydrated food, you might think of astronauts eating meals out of a plastic bag. In reality, dehydrated food is great for everyone. Dehydrated food is much easier to store than canned food because it takes up less space, and it is particularly useful for emergency food storage. The beauty of dehydrated food is that it is highly versatile – you can use a dehydrator (or your oven) to dehydrate everything from fruits and vegetables to meat, herbs, grains and more.

Drying your food at home can help mitigate some of the lost nutrients. The actual losses associated with home drying are minimal, but be aware the more heat and light the food is exposed to, the more pronounced the losses become. The best drying methods expose foods to minimal heat and finish the drying process in as short a time as possible. Store dried foods out of the light to avoid degradation during storage.

Foods dried right after being harvested will maintain the most nutrients because they won't have time to lose a lot of nutrients to processes other than the drying process itself. If you raise and harvest your produce, you'll have a lot more control over how soon it is set out to dry. There's no telling how long it's been since the foods sitting on your local grocery store's shelves were harvested, so it's tough to judge how much nutrients have been lost.

Dehydrating food is not difficult, but there are a few things you need to know before you try it for yourself. Below you will find a collection of tips to help you get the most out of your food dehydration:

1. Always start with high-quality ingredients – choose ripe, unbruised fruits and vegetables and fresh meats.

2. Prepare your food items in the way you want them to be served. For example, if you want to make apple chips, then you need to slice the apple – you won't be able to dehydrate a whole apple and then slice it.

3. Try to keep your ingredients uniform in size and thickness to ensure even drying – slices should only be 1/8 to ¼ inch thickness at the

most.

4. Wash foods before preparing for dehydration – this applies to fruits, vegetables, and herbs.

5. If you want to keep fruits and vegetables from browning, brush them with lemon juice. Blanching or lightly steaming vegetables may also help.

6. Maintain a stable temperature in your food dehydrator between 130°F and 140°F with constant air circulation.

7. Once your food is properly dried you should store it immediately in an air-tight container once it has cooled. Store your containers in a cool, dark location.

8. Check your stored food periodically to make sure that it is still dry – the food may spoil if it is exposed to moisture.

Are you fairly sure you want to try a dehydrator, but not sure about forking over the money?

Consider these benefits of using a dehydrator:

- You can save money dehydrating your foods. Buy vegetables, for example, when they are plentiful and less expensive, and use those dehydrated foods until the next harvest season.

- You can extend the shelf life of foods. Making your fresh fruits will give you fruits that last for up to a year.

- Dehydrators are reliable and easy to use. They're really simple to use, and they rarely break down for years after their purchase.

- Dehydrators are pretty much foolproof. Since the temperatures you use will be low, it's difficult to leave food in for too long and over-dehydrate it.

- You can make healthy foods. Purchase locally grown bulk food and preserve it. You'll still be feeding your family real, healthy food.

- You'll be prepared for emergencies. No, I'm not talking about zombies. It's just good to have food stored for power outages and "rainy days".

Rehydrating Dehydrated Foods and Meals

Recipes for dehydrating foods and meals do not generally include the instructions to rehydrate them when you're ready to use them. I will provide you with simple steps that can be used whenever you rehydrate foods.

1. Choose the agent you'll use for rehydrating. It may be just water, or broth or juice. It depends on what you're rehydrating.
2. Fill your chosen rehydrating container with the liquid you'll be using to rehydrate your food. A bit too much water won't hurt your dried foods.
3. Check the temperature of your rehydrating fluid. You won't want it too hot. Some foods react poorly to hot water. Soak the dried food, leaving it for whatever time it needs to rehydrate fully.
4. Check on the rehydrating foods frequently. Don't remove it from water if it has an odd taste or a leathery feel.
5. Sometimes you can rehydrate as you cook a dried dish, like when you make soup. The meat and vegetables can be added as it cooks. The foods will rehydrate as your soup is cooking.

Chapter 1:

Simple Dehydration

Simple Dehydration Food

Dehydration is a simple and ancient means of preserving food. Drying food was a way to save and store harvests of fruit, grains, and vegetables. Laying out food on mats to dry under the sun morphed into hand-built dehydrator boxes with mesh trays. Once ovens with reliably consistent temperatures existed, food was dried on oven trays. Some people still use ovens for dehydration, and if your oven has a minimum temperature setting of lower than 170°F and convection air, you may be able to use it for dehydrating food. Now we have the convenience of electric dehydrators that offer several improvements over other methods. Different types of foods require specific temperatures for food safety and the most efficient drying times. Circulating air prompts faster drying times as well.

Equipment

Dehydration is mostly about prep work, so having the appropriate tools will make your job easier. Make sure you have the following tools on hand.

Baking sheet

If you don't already have one, a good-quality baking sheet that disperses heat properly and doesn't buckle under high heat is a great addition to your kitchen. Use it for roasting vegetables and fish.

Blender

Blenders are great for making purées for sauces, soups, and fruit leather. A food processor or immersion blender also works for this purpose.

Four-cup measuring pitcher

These pitchers are good for measuring liquids and for measuring the yield of dehydrated foods (if you don't have a kitchen scale).

Kitchen knife

Aside from the dehydrator itself, a kitchen knife is the most important tool for dehydrating. A good knife will make your prep work much easier. Perhaps you already have a favorite knife—one that keeps a good edge, has a straight blade, and is comfortable to hold for extended periods. Good knives don't need to be expensive. In our kitchen we use the same knives many culinary schools offer; they are inexpensive but great tools for the job.

Kitchen scale

An inexpensive digital scale is very useful for measuring ingredients with precision and is also helpful for measuring and portioning the completed and dehydrated meals.

Parchment paper

Line baking sheets with parchment paper to prevent food from sticking to the pan. It also makes for easy cleanup.

Mandoline

This is an excellent tool for making precise and consistent slices. Consistency is a key factor in proper dehydration. If you need a veggie to be cut to a ¼-inch thickness, a mandoline is an easy way to ensure that consistency.

Vacuum Sealer

This is an excellent gadget for preparing your dehydrated food for long-term storage. A vacuum sealer removes most of the oxygen from the stored food, which prolongs its shelf life.

Why Dehydration Food (save money, space, clean eating etc....)

Do you want to save your favorite food from rotting by preserving it and making it available whenever you need it? Imagine preserving your whole kitchen garden in a compact size without using any unnatural and unhealthy preservatives and additives. It seems implausible, but as you continue to read this book, you will get to know all the dehydrating secrets and techniques for dehydrating foods.

It's Cost-Effective

The primary benefit of dehydrated food is its cost-effectiveness. The longer shelf life results in saving money by not sending it down the drain because of rottenness. Dehydrated foods can last for years without electricity to keep the food cool; hence, it is a high energy saving process too.

Retained Nutritional Values

As compared to other preserving methods such as freezing or canning, dehydration retains maximum dietary benefits. They are more calories' dense food meaning there is a big difference between 1 ounce of dried kiwis and 1 ounce of fresh kiwis.

A Major Space-Saver

Dehydration reduces food size and weight considerably, allowing you to store extra food in a compact space.

A Snack In A Snap

Dehydrated foods can serve as healthy snacks that you can have any time a need arises. Moreover, you can add dried fruits and vegetables in a plethora of meals and dishes to give them a creative touch and amaze your family and guests at the same time.

Types of Dehydrator

Ascorbic Acid or Vitamin C Bath

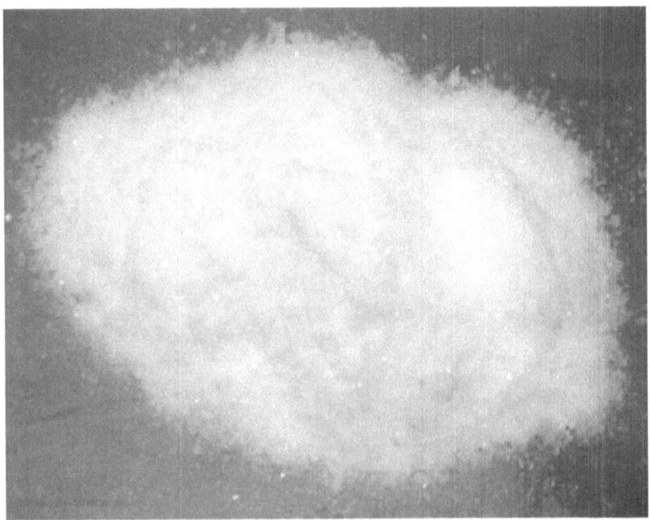

By soaking fruits or soft vegetables in an ascorbic acid solution (one-part of ascorbic acid in 1 gallon of water) immediately after cutting will stop discoloring and browning. An exception is leafy greens, herbs, and broccoli as the acid will discolor them severely. For this, soak the cut fruits immediately in the solution for 8 to 10 minutes. Drain for dehydration.

Skin Cracking

Fruits with tougher skins such as plums, cherries, grapes, figs, or berries may need their skins to be cracked before dehydration to pull moisture out from the fruit properly. For this, boil a pot of water and dip the fruit in it for 15 seconds. Remove and dip them in ice-cold water immediately. Drain water entirely before drying them.

Blanching

It is a process used for scalding vegetables in boiling water or steam, to stop the enzymatic action within the vegetables. Be cautious about the timing, as over blanching results in loss of nutrients and under blanching can cause food spoilage during or after the dehydration. For blanching, usually, two methods are used: boiling vegetables in water for some time, and scalding vegetables above the boiling water level, also known as steam blanching — steam from the boiling water scalds the vegetables.

Citric Acid bath

Citric Acid kills bacteria and stops food discoloration. For this, mix a teaspoon of citric acid in 2.5 cups of water, or you can mix equal parts of water and lemon juice. Soak the food for 8 to 10 minutes and drain entirely before dehydration.

Storage

Dehydrated foods can last for years if stored properly. To ensure maximum shelf life, you need to prevent dried food from moisture, heat, microorganism, light and oxygen. Essential steps of storage are:

Cooling

When the fruit is dry enough, remove it from the dehydrator and cool the fruit completely in a cool and dry place for half an hour; storing warm food will reintroduce moisture due to condensation. Make sure not to leave the dried food for too long as it will also result in moisture to come back into the food.

Conditioning

To ensure even distribution of moisture within the food, place the dried food in loose packaging and seal it for 2 to 4 days.

Packaging

As a final step of storage, you need to pack your dehydrated food in air-tight jars or cans. Store your jars or containers in a cool, dark, and dry place to maximize the shelf-life.

Rehydration

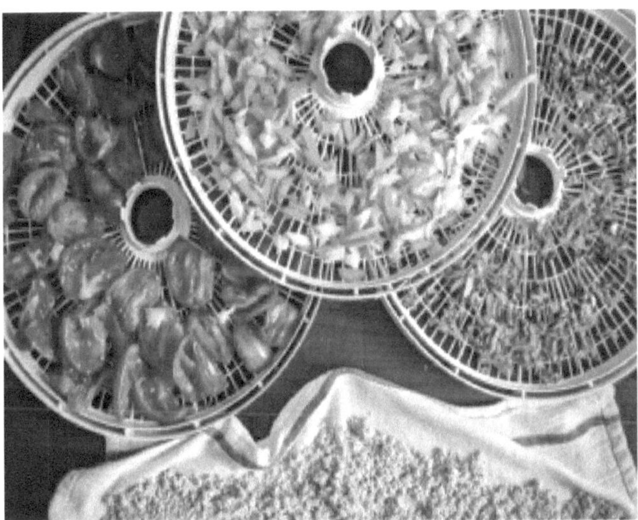

Water is life. So, rehydration is giving back life to the dehydrated product. Dried food changes back to its original plump and soft shape when we rehydrate them as we are adding back the moisture we removed during dehydration. Usually, we need to rehydrate food when we want to eat or cook dried food with other ingredients. We can rehydrate via several methods such as:

Brief Soaking

We can rehydrate some food by a quick dip in boiling water for less than 10 seconds. For instance, spinach and collard greens.

Extended Soaking

Mostly fruits and vegetables require a 15-minute soak in a covered pan of boiling water. Do it before using them in cooking while preparing the other items on the ingredients' list.

Rehydration by Refrigeration

It takes much longer, hence, an ideal method to use when you need your dehydrated items ready before you get home from work. For this, put 1 cup of dehydrated food in a jar and fill it to the top with hot water. Put the jar in the refrigerator for up to 24 hours.

Chapter 2:

Basic Dehydration

Basic Method

You can start drying products that are already available in your kitchen.

Essential drying process:

1. Food
2. A source of heat
3. You needed trays or racks to use in drying the food on. The trays that should be used is slotted wood or mesh trays. You have to avoid using solid trays because this can block air from circulating around your food. Cover it using a wood frame with cheesecloth and use it as a drying rack.
4. Containers to store the food in.

Those are all you need to get started drying your food. There are other items you can use for easier way, but these items are the only absolute necessities.

Avoid trays that are made from the following materials because they can add harmful substances to your food during the drying process:

1. Fiberglass
2. Vinyl
3. Aluminum
4. Copper
5. Plastic
6. Galvanized metal

The following are not essential but can help you dehydrate food easier:

1. A commercial food dehydrator
2. A fan
3. A blancher

4. A sulfur box
5. A scale
6. A thermometer

Temperature and Cooking Time To Dry Food

Experience will help answer this question. There are many factors that will influence the time needed to dry a food, they are:

1. The water content of the food
2. The sugar content of the food
3. The size of the piece of food (thick or thin slices)
4. The amount of air circulation as the food is being dried
5. The level of humidity in the air entering the dehydrator
6. The air temperature inside the dehydrator
7. The type of dehydrator being used

In general, the lower the air temperature inside the dehydrator, the longer the drying time. The air temperature should be high enough to draw moisture from the food but not high enough to cook it. Temperatures that are too low might allow the food to spoil and temperatures that are too high may cause the surface area of the food to harden and prevent moisture from escaping.

The three categories of food, meat, fish, fruits and vegetables and herbs all require different drying temperatures:

1. Meats & Fish: 145 degrees Fahrenheit & above
2. Fruits & Vegetables: 130 to 140 degrees Fahrenheit
3. Herbs & Flowers: 100 to 110 degrees Fahrenheit

Nutrition

The dehydrated foods you buy in the store have a fraction of the nutritional value of the foods you dry yourself. The industrial process of drying large amounts of food is harsh—and that's not to mention the chemicals and preservatives used.

Here's an example to show just how much of the good stuff is eliminated: A cup of fresh apricots contains almost three times as much vitamin A as a cup of commercially dried apricots. The vitamin C present in fresh apricots is completely gone by the time the commercial drying process is complete, and the fiber has been cut in half.

In addition to the nutrients, sweeteners are added most of the time. The manufacturers know people like sweet foods and will add sugar to dried fruits even though they don't need it. They almost always add it too tart fruits like cranberries to sweeten them up and have been known to add it to fruits that don't need it to make them sweeter.

The harsh chemicals and processes used to dry food on a production line rapidly are much harder on your diet than the dry air used at home. While a small amount of the nutrients will be lost, it isn't enough to be concerned with. A carefully controlled environment should be used to dry your foods not to lose the nutrients.

Specific vitamins are more susceptible to lose during the drying process than others.

Vitamin C is water-soluble, and some are lost in the water as it dries and evaporates. On the other hand, vitamin A is retained during the dehydration process. Fiber is unaffected by home drying, as are most minerals.

Once dried, store your dried food in a cool, dark place. Certain foods begin to break down and lose nutrients when exposed to light for any given period.

There is one thing you need to keep in mind when consuming dehydrated foods:

When you're eating them, you're eating compact versions of more substantial foods.

The compact versions have the same amount of sugar and equal number of calories in a smaller package. You're still getting close to the same amount of nutrients in the smaller box, so there's no need to eat more to make up for it.

Chapter 3:

Dehydrator Foods

Dehydrators perform a simple operation: A fan and motor circulate heated air through the machine, which results in the removal of moisture from the food on the dehydrator trays. Foods with high water content, such as bell peppers, take longer to dehydrate than foods with a lower water content, such as kale. Likewise, food with a high density, such as a large bean, will take longer to dry than food with a lower density, such as rice.

To get the best results when dehydrating the recipes, pay close attention to the directions for prepping the vegetables. If the recipe calls for cutting the vegetables into ½-inch dice, be sure to cut them to that size so they will dehydrate at the same rate as the rest of the recipe. If you are uncertain what ½-inch dice looks like, measure and cut a piece to that size and set it aside as a guide. Cutting larger pieces than is called for is easy to do by accident, and that will affect how the recipe itself turns out, the drying time, and the consistency of the food.

When food comes out of the dehydrator, it looks vastly different from its original state. Hummus and soups can look as cracked and dried as a desert floor. Food can come off the trays in thin sheets, which you can break into smaller pieces. Properly dried pieces of fruit bend but don't break, and they do not feel moist when you squeeze them. Other foods—vegetables, grains, and legumes—should be hard and dry.

It is possible to burned the food in a dehydrator, so pay attention to both the temperature and timing recommendations given in the recipes. Also, when you're learning how to dehydrate food, be sure to check the food every few hours. You may need to rotate the trays to ensure that the food dries evenly, and if you find that part of your recipe is dry before the rest, remove that part and store it. In contrast, the rest of the recipe continues to dry.

Pre-treating Foods

Skin Cracking

Fruits and berries with tough skins may need to have the skins cracked before the drying process to allow moisture to be pulled from within the fruit.

Here are steps required to crack skins:

1. Bring a pot of water to a boil.
2. Dip fruit into the boiling water for 15 seconds.
3. Remove from boiling water and immediately dip in ice-cold water.
4. Drain water off fruit before drying.

Ascorbic Acid (Vitamin C)

Ascorbic acid is a fancy name for vitamin C. This treatment is used to keep fruit from darkening while drying and kills more bacteria than regular drying alone. It adds vitamin C to the fruit and helps offset any losses of vitamin C associated with the drying process.

You can create an ascorbic acid bath for your food using one of the following techniques:

1. Pure ascorbic acid crystals can be purchased from most supermarkets. Mix 2 tablespoons of the crystals into a quart of water.

2. Crush up 12 vitamin C tablets and dissolve in a quart of water.

As you cut the fruit, submerse it in the bath for 8 to 10 minutes. Drain the solution from the fruit and it's ready to go in the dehydrator.

Citric Acid Bath

The citric acid bath is similar to the ascorbic acid bath, in that it's used to prevent darkening and to kill bacteria.

To create the bath, you can add a teaspoon of citric acid to 2 1/2 cups of water or you can mix equal parts water and lemon juice.

Let it sit for 8 to minutes and drain the liquid off the fruit and you're good to go.

Sulphur Treatment

Sulphur has been used for hundreds of years to treat many different foods. It's traditionally been used to keep foods from spoiling during the drying process and to prevent discoloration.

You can use it at home if you want to. Make sure you purchase food grade sodium metabisulfite if you plan on adding it to your food. All it takes is a single tablespoon stirred into a quart of water to treat produce. Soak it for 8 to 10 minutes and make sure you drain it off before drying.

I've seen some recipes that call for use of burning Sulphur. This is an arcane method and it can negatively impact your health and the health of those around you. Avoid this method in favor of one of the safer methods on this list. If you do decide to use burning Sulphur, do it outdoors in a well-ventilated area.

Dehydrator Fruits

Fruit is one of the easiest foods to dry, so it's where most people start when trying to learn the ins and outs of dehydration. It's a good way to preserve extra produce and allows you to buy it when it's at its cheapest during the local harvest season.

Selecting the Best Fruit

The fruit you buy is critical part of the process. It's important you select only the freshest, ripest fruits. For this reason, it isn't a good idea to buy your fruit from most grocery stores. By the time fruit (and vegetables, for that matter) hits grocery store shelves, it's usually at or near the end of its life cycle. A much better option is to get your produce from a local farmer's market or straight from a local farm.

You want food that's at the peak of its maturity. Underdeveloped produce will be lacking in both color and flavor. Older produce will be too ripe and will be too sweet and squishy after drying.

Don't use damaged fruit. Make sure you select fruit that's free of decay, bruises and cuts or scrapes that compromise quality. It's important to keep in mind that drying fruit isn't going to make fruit that going bad more edible. It's just going to make bad dried fruit.

To test your fruit, pull pieces from various areas of the drying device. Cut the pieces in half and squeeze the fruit. If you're able to squeeze liquid from the fruit, it isn't dry enough. The fruit shouldn't be sticky to the touch.

Cooling, Conditioning and Packaging

Once you're confident the fruit is done drying, you're going to be tempted to package it and be done with it. There are still a couple important steps left before you're finished. It's time to start the cooling and conditioning process.

First, cool the fruit by letting it sit out in a cool, dark place for a half hour to an hour. You don't want to package your food warm because it can reintroduce moisture into the food due to condensation. Be careful not to leave your fruit out for too long because that can also cause moisture to get back into the fruit. The last step in the conditioning process is to take the dried fruit and place it in loose packaging. Seal it up and let it sit for a week.

Dehydrator Vegetables

Dried vegetables are great for making soups and stews and can be used as garnish for many food dishes. You can reintroduce water to some dried vegetables and they'll return to a form similar to what they were before drying.

Avoid drying vegetables with a strong taste or odor with other fruits or vegetables at the same time. The strong-scented vegetables will impart some of their scent to the weaker vegetables and the taste may even be transferred. Do you know what garlic-flavored banana chips taste like? Trust me, you don't want to find out. Learn from my mistakes.

Blanching

Vegetables need to be blanched to kill enzymes. The blanching process involves either steaming or boiling vegetable for a certain time to ensure the harmful enzymes have been deactivated. Most vegetables need to be blanched. I'd go ahead and blanch them just to be safe. It isn't going to change the taste and texture and it safeguards you against harmful enzymes.

Preparation

After blanching, drain the vegetables and slice them into pieces the size you want to dry.

Cooling, Conditioning and Packaging

Vegetables are done drying when they're brittle to the touch. Cool vegetables for 24 hours.

Since vegetables are dried until they're brittle, there's no need to condition them like you have to condition fruit. Once vegetables are cool, they're ready for packaging.

Dehydrator Herbs and Spices

Many exotic spices, including cinnamon, nutmeg, and cloves, can't be grown in the Northeastern United States without a prohibitively expensive artificial climate. But a host of herbs that are commonly used for spicing or herbal tea are fast to grow. This includes, among other things, mints, basil, oregano, tarragon, rosemary, chamomile, anise, borage, caraway, dill, thyme, cilantro, fennel, lavage, herb, and savory season.

I have two beds on my mini-farm dedicated to growing herbs. I do so because certain herbs, such as lemon verbena, are best used fresh, but also because growing and drying for culinary use of my herbs and teas save a lot of money. Just a few ounces of dried basil or tarragon cost a lot at my local supermarket. Since I like to use a lot of herbs in my meals, growing my herbs and drying them adds to my bottom line.

Selecting Herbs for Dehydrating

With this, the most important rule is the same as the most important rule about what you would grow in a garden, or what vegetables you can dehydrate: just grow and dehydrate the herbs you want. Experimenting with stuff that you have never done before makes sense, just in case you want it. But if you don't like basil, it is a waste of time dehydrating a bunch of it.

Generally speaking, you want herbs to be harvested during their most vigorous growth, and before they set seed so that they are sweeter. When you pick them early in the morning before the sun volatilizes the essential oils they have stored throughout the night, you can also get more flavor.

Preparing Herbs for Dehydrating

Regardless of the countless birds flying over and mice roaming about, herbs need to be washed thoroughly before drying. When picked, herbs should

the desired portion of the plant. This will usually be leaves, but it will be flowers in the case of other plants, such as chamomile. Simply cut the desired portion of the plant off the stem, but don't remove any more leaves or flowers.

Dehydrating Herbs

The active herbal principles are generally, but not always, essential oils which can be easily pushed away by excess heat. Even with herbs, whose flavor is primarily a result of non-volatile elements, excess heat sometimes contributes to bitterness. The herbs should also be dried at temperatures that do not exceed 115 degrees Fahrenheit. Place herbs in the dehydrator on a fine-meshed sheet, and leave until they become crisp.

Storing Herbs

Herbs are better sliced, dried, or powdered right before use. You will see a tremendous difference if you have ever compared freshly milled pepper from a pepper mill to that from a can in the grocery store. The same is true for every herb or spice.

Being fragile, the dried herbs should be stored for protection in a rigid jar. Vacuum sealing is not practical, because it will convert dried herbs into powder. You do want to store herbs to give as little space as possible for oxygen. So, I consider using the smallest available canning jars, which are usually 8 ounces or 1/2-pint jars. Sunlight ravages plants, so keep them hidden from the sun. Heat can cause unnecessary flavor changes as well as the loss of flavor components, so store them in a cool place as well.

Chapter 4: Simple Recipes

1. Homemade Chili Powder

Preparation Time: 10 minutes

Cooking Time: 6 hours 15 minutes

Servings: 24

Ingredients:

12 red chili peppers

Directions:

Place ParaFlexx Screens on the racks of your Excalibur Food Dehydrator. Carefully slice the chili peppers into thin strips. Note: The amount of heat in your chili powder will depend on how much pith and seed you allow to stay with the peppers. If you want super-hot powder keep the seeds and pith. For less spicy powder discard most of the seeds and pith. Lay the peppers (and seeds and pith if desired) on the screens and set your Excalibur to 115F. Dehydrate for about 5 to 6 hours or until the peppers are completely dried. Transfer the contents of your Excalibur to a blender and pulse until a rough powder form. Store in jars or zipper lock bags.

Nutrition:

Calories: 24

Fat: 1 gram

Carbs: 4 grams

Protein: 1 gram

2. Spicy Carrot Powder

Preparation Time: 15 minutes

Cooking Time: 6 hours 15 minutes

Servings: 12

Ingredients:

6 large carrots, peeled, chopped

2 jalapeño peppers, sliced

1 tablespoon salt

Directions:

Place the carrots in a food processor. Pulse until the carrots are roughly chopped but not a puree.

Place ParaFlexx Screens on the racks of your Excalibur Food Dehydrator and use all but one rack for the carrots. Make sure the carrots are in thin even layers not thicker than 1/4 inch.

Use one rack for the jalapeño peppers. Set your Excalibur to 150F and dehydrate for 6 hours or until the carrots are completely dry.

Transfer the dried carrots and jalapeños to a blender and blend until you get a fine powder. Store in jars or zipper lock bags.

Nutrition:

Calories: 40

Fat: 0 gram

Carbs: 9 grams

Protein: 1 gram

3. Beef Jerky

Preparation Time: 30 minutes

Cooking Time: 4 hours

Servings: 4

Ingredients:

2 lbs. London broil, sliced thinly

1 teaspoon sesame oil

3/4 teaspoon garlic powder

1 teaspoon onion powder

3 tablespoon Brown sugar

3 tablespoon Soy sauce

Directions:

Add all ingredients except meat in the large zip-lock bag and mix until well combined. Add meat in bag. Seal bag and massage gently to cover the meat with marinade. Let marinate the meat for 30 minutes. Arrange marinated meat slices in a single layer on the dehydrator racks and dehydrate at 160 F/ 71 C for 4 hours.

Nutrition:

Calories: 347

Fat: 11.2 grams

Carbs: 8.4 grams

Protein: 51.1 grams

4. Chicken Jerky

Preparation Time: 10 minutes

Cooking Time: 7 hours

Servings: 4

Ingredients:

1 ½ lb. chicken tenders, boneless, skinless and cut into ¼ inch strips

¼ teaspoon ground ginger

¼ teaspoon black pepper

½ teaspoon garlic powder

1 teaspoon lemon juice

½ cup soy sauce

Directions:

Mix all ingredients except chicken into the zip-lock bag.

Add chicken and seal bag and mix until chicken is well coated. Place in refrigerator for 30 minutes.

Arrange marinated meat slices of dehydrator trays and dehydrate at 145 F/ 63 C for 6-7 hours.

Nutrition:

Calories: 342

Fat: 12.6 grams

Carbs: 2.9 grams

Protein: 51.3 grams

5. Ranch Beef Jerky

Preparation Time: 15 minutes

Cooking Time: 8 hours

Serving: 6

Ingredients:

2 lbs. flank steak, cut into thin slices

¼ teaspoon cayenne pepper

1 ½ teaspoon liquid smoke

2 tablespoon red pepper flakes

3 tablespoon ranch seasoning

¾ cup Worcestershire sauce

¾ cup soy sauce

Directions:

Add all ingredients into the large mixing bowl and mix well. Cover bowl and place in refrigerator for overnight.

Arrange marinated meat slices on dehydrator racks and dehydrate at 145 F/ 63 C for 7-8 hours.

Nutrition:

Calories: 346

Fat: 12.9 grams

Carbs: 9.5 grams

Protein: 44.3 grams

6. Turkey Jerky

Preparation Time: 15 minutes

Cooking Time: 5 hours

Serving: 4

Ingredients:

1 lb. turkey meat, cut into thin slices

1 teaspoon salt

2 teaspoon garlic powder

1 tbsp. onion powder

2 teaspoon brown sugar

1/3 cup Worcestershire sauce

¼ teaspoon Tabasco sauce

2 tbsps. Soy sauce

1 tbsp. liquid smoke

Directions:

Add all ingredients except meat in the large zip-lock bag and mix until well combined.

Add meat in bag. Seal bag and massage gently to cover the meat with marinade. Place in refrigerator for overnight.

Arrange marinated meat slices on the dehydrator racks and dehydrate at 160 F/ 71 C for 5 hours.

Nutrition:

Calories: 233

Fat: 5.7 grams

Carbs: 8.5 grams

Protein: 34.1 grams

7. Tofu Jerky

Preparation Time: 10 minutes

Cooking Time: 4 hours

Servings: 4

Ingredients:

1 block tofu, pressed

4 drops liquid smoke

2 tbsps. Worcestershire sauce

2 tbsps. Sriracha

Directions:

Cut tofu in half then cut into the slices.

In a bowl, mix liquid smoke, Worcestershire sauce, and sriracha.

Add tofu slices in a bowl and mix until well coated with marinade. Cover bowl tightly and place in refrigerator for overnight.

Place marinated tofu slices on the dehydrator trays and dehydrate at 145 F/ 63 C for 4 hours.

Nutrition:

Calories: 44

Fat: 1.8 grams

Carbs: 3.9 grams

Protein: 3.2 grams

8. Sweet & Spicy Beef Jerky

Preparation Time: 15 minutes

Cooking Time: 6 hours

Servings: 8

Ingredients:

2 lbs. flank steak, trimmed fat and sliced into thin strips

1 teaspoon red pepper flakes

1 teaspoon liquid smoke

1 teaspoon garlic powder

1 teaspoon onion powder

2 teaspoon black pepper

1 tablespoon brown sugar

2/3 cup soy sauce

2/3 cup Worcestershire sauce

Directions:

Add red pepper flakes, liquid smoke, garlic powder, onion powder, black pepper, brown sugar, soy sauce, and Worcestershire sauce in a large zip-lock bag and mix well.

Add sliced meat in the zip-lock bag. Seal the bag well and shake until meat is well coated. Place in refrigerator for overnight.

Arrange marinated meat slices on dehydrator rack and dehydrate at 160 F/ 71 C for 5-6 hours.

Store in air-tight container.

Nutrition:

Calories: 260

Fat: 9.5 grams

Carbs: 7.7 grams

Protein: 33.1 grams

9. Sweet & Smoky Salmon Jerky

Preparation Time: 15 minutes

Cooking Time: 5 hours

Servings: 6

Ingredients:

2 lbs. salmon, sliced in strips

3 teaspoon black pepper

3 tablespoon smoked sea salt

¼ cup liquid smoke

2 tablespoon black pepper

1 cup brown sugar

1 cup soy sauce

1 orange juice

Directions:

Add all ingredients except salmon slices into the large bowl and mix well.

Add sliced salmon in the bowl and mix until well coated. Cover bowl and place in refrigerator for overnight.

Arrange marinated salmon slices in a single layer on the dehydrator racks and dehydrate at 160 F/ 71 C for 5 hours.

Nutrition:

Calories: 329

Fat: 9.5 grams

Carbs: 30.5 grams

Protein: 32.5 grams

10. Lemon Salmon Jerky

Preparation Time: 15 minutes

Cooking Time: 4 hours

Servings: 6

Ingredients:

1 ¼ lbs. salmon, cut into ¼ inch slices

1/2 teaspoon liquid smoke

1 ¼ teaspoon black pepper

1 ½ tablespoon fresh lemon juice

1 tablespoon molasses

½ cup soy sauce, low sodium

Directions:

In a bowl, mix liquid smoke, black pepper, lemon juice, molasses, and soy sauce.

Add sliced salmon into the bowl and mix until well coated. Cover bowl and place in refrigerator for overnight.

Strain sliced salmon in colander and pat dry with paper towel.

Arrange sliced salmon on a dehydrator tray and dehydrate at 145 F/ 63 C for 3-4 hours.

Nutrition:

Calories: 148

Fat: 5.9 grams

Carbs: 4.5 grams

Protein: 19.7 grams

11. Perfect Lamb Jerky

Preparation Time: 10 minutes

Cooking Time: 6 hours

Servings: 6

Ingredients:

2 ½ lbs. boneless lamb, trimmed fat and slice into thin strips

½ teaspoon black pepper

1 tablespoon oregano

1 teaspoon garlic powder

1 ½ teaspoon onion powder

3 tablespoon Worcestershire sauce

1/3 cup soy sauce

Directions:

Add soy sauce, Worcestershire sauce, onion powder, garlic powder, oregano, and black pepper in the large bowl and mix well.

Add meat slices in the bowl and mix until well coated. Cover bowl tightly and place in refrigerator for overnight.

Arrange marinated meat slices on dehydrator racks and dehydrate to 145 F/ 63 C for 5-6 hours.

Nutrition:

Calories: 373

Fat: 14 grams

Carbs: 4 grams

Protein: 54.2 grams

12. Tasty Pineapple Chunks

Preparation Time: 10 minutes

Cooking time: 12 hours

Serving: 4

Ingredient:

1 ripe pineapple

Directions:

Peel and cut pineapple. Cut in half and then cut in ¼ inch thick chunks.

Place pineapple chunks on dehydrator racks and dehydrate at 135 F/ 58 C for 12 hours.

Nutrition:

Calories: 62

Fat: 0.2 grams

Carbs: 16.2 grams

Protein: 0.7 grams

13. Dried Mango

Preparation Time: 5 Minutes

Cooking Time: 8 Hours

Serving: 2

Ingredients:

½ mango, peeled, pitted, and cut into ⅜-inch slices

Directions:

Arrange the mango slices flat in a single layer in the Cook & Crisp Basket. Place in the pot and close the Crisping Lid.

Press Dehydrate, set the temperature to 135°F, and set the time to 8 hours. Select Start/Stop to begin.

When dehydrating is complete, remove the basket from the pot and transfer the mango slices to an airtight container.

Nutrition:

Calories: 67

Fat: 0 gram

Carbs: 18 grams

Protein: 1 gram

14. Chia Seed Pudding

Preparation Time: 10 minutes

Cooking Time: 0

Serving: 3

Ingredients:

2 cups of unsweetened almond milk

1 tablespoon of raw honey

½ cup of chia seeds

½ cup fresh blueberries

Directions:

In a large bowl, add the almond milk, chia seeds, maple syrup, and vanilla extract and stir to combine well. Refrigerate for at least 3-4 hours, stirring occasionally. Serve with the topping of strawberry slices.

Nutrition:

Calories: 139

Fat: 9.1 grams

Carbs: 18.6 grams

Protein: 4.9 grams

15. Bacon Jerky

Preparation Time: 15 minutes

Cooking Time: 5 hours

Servings: 4

Ingredients:

1 lb. thick cut bacon

1 teaspoon black pepper

1 tablespoon brown sugar

1 teaspoon chili powder

Directions:

Place the strips of bacon on baking sheets. In a small bowl, combine the pepper, sugar, and chili powder. Season the bacon strips with the spice blend and allow to sit for 10 minutes.

Set your Excalibur to 165F and arrange the bacon on the racks.

Dehydrate for 5 hours. Make sure all of the bacon is evenly dehydrated before removing from the racks

Nutrition:

Calories: 38

Fat: 2.1 grams

Carbs: 3 grams

Protein: 1.9 grams

16. Ham Jerky

Preparation Time: 1 hour

Cooking Time: 4 hours

Servings: 4

Ingredients:

1 lb. sliced ham

4 tablespoons soy sauce

4 tablespoons water

1 teaspoon pepper

1/2 teaspoon onion powder

Directions:

In a large bowl combine the soy sauce, water, pepper, and onion powder. Add the ham slices and turn to coat. Allow the ham to marinate for 1 hour.

Remove the ham from the bowl and remove excess marinade. Set your Excalibur Food Dehydrator to 165F and place the ham strips evenly on the racks.

Dehydrate for 4 hours and make sure the ham is evenly dehydrated before removing from the racks.

Nutrition:

Calories: 196

Fat: 9.8 grams

Carbs: 6.1 grams

Protein: 19.9 grams

17. Simple Apple Leather

Preparation Time: 5 minutes

Cooking Time: 6 hours

Servings: 12

Ingredients:

8 cups applesauce

1 3oz. box sugar free jello

Directions:

In a large bowl, combine the apple sauce and Jello. Place ParaFlexx Screens on the racks of your Excalibur and pour the puree onto the screens. Use a spatula to spread the puree about 1/8 inch thick evenly.

Set your Excalibur to 140F and dehydrate for 6 hours. Make sure the leather is completely dehydrated and not sticky before removing from the screens.

Nutrition:

Calories: 103

Fat: 0.1 gram

Carbs: 18.4 grams

Protein: 3.6 grams

18. Mirepoix Powder

Preparation Time: 20 minutes

Cooking Time: 6 hours

Servings: 24

Ingredients:

2 yellow onions, thinly sliced

3 carrots, sliced into thin rounds

3 stalks celery, cut into thin slices

Directions:

Place ParaFlexx Screens on the racks of your Excalibur Food Dehydrator. On separate racks place layers of onion, carrot, and celery. Make sure they are even layers.

Set your Excalibur to 150F and dehydrate for 6 hours.

When the vegetables are completely dehydrated, place them in a blender together. Blend until a fine powder form. Store the powder in jars and use as the base for many soups and sauces.

Nutrition:

Calories: 7

Fat: 0 gram

Carbs: 1.7 grams

Protein: 0.2 grams

19. Int Leaves

Preparation Time: 10 minutes

Cooking Time: 6 hours 10 minutes

Servings: 12

Ingredients:

2 bunches fresh peppermint

Directions:

The leaves on the rack of your Excalibur Food Dehydrator and set to 150F. Dehydrate for 6 hours.

Remove mint leaves from the racks and store in jars or zipper lock bags until ready to use.

Nutrition:

Calories: 96

Fat: 0 gram

Carbs: 24 grams

Protein: 0 gram

20. Zucchini Chips

Preparation Time: 20 minutes

Cooking Time: 12 hours 10 minutes

Servings: 6

Ingredients:

4 zucchinis, sliced thin

Juice from 2 lemons

1 teaspoon salt

Directions:

Combine the zucchini strips, lemon juice, and salt, and stir to coat.

Place the zucchini strips on the racks of your Excalibur Food Dehydrator in a single layer.

Set the Excalibur to 115F and dehydrate for 12 hours or until the zucchini strips are crispy.

Nutrition:

Calories: 25

Fat: 0.3 grams

Carbs: 5.8 grams

Protein: 1.7 grams

21. Pumpkin Chips

Preparation Time: 15 minutes

Cooking Time: 18 hours 10 minutes

Servings: 6

Ingredients:

1 pumpkin

2 tablespoons coconut oil, melted

1 teaspoon cinnamon

1 teaspoon nutmeg

Directions:

Remove the seeds, pulp, and skin from the pumpkin, and slice the pumpkin flesh into thin slices.

Try to make the slices no more than 1/8 inch thick.

In a large bowl, combine the pumpkin slices, coconut oil, cinnamon, nutmeg, and salt. Stir well to coat.

Place the pumpkin slices on the racks of your Excalibur and set to 125F. Dehydrated for 18 hours or until the slices are crispy.

Nutrition:

Calories: 140

Fat: 8 grams

Carbs: 16 grams

Protein: 2 grams

22. Eggplant Chips

Preparation Time: 30 minutes

Cooking Time: 6 hours 15 minutes

Servings: 6

Ingredients:

4 baby eggplants, sliced thin

3 tablespoons olive oil

1/2 teaspoon smoked paprika

1/2 teaspoon oregano

1/4 teaspoon cayenne pepper

2 tablespoons salt

Directions:

In a large bowl, combine the eggplant slices olive oil, paprika, oregano, cayenne pepper, and salt.

Place the eggplant slices on the racks of your Excalibur and set to 135F.

Dehydrate for 5 to 6 hours or until eggplant slices are entirely dried and crispy.

Nutrition:

Calories: 35

Fat: 1 gram

Carbs: 8 grams

Protein: 1 gram

23. Crunch Green Bean Chips

Preparation Time: 15 minutes

Cooking Time: 12 hours 10 minutes

Servings: 12

Ingredients:

3 lbs. Fresh green beans

1/4 cup coconut oil, melted

1 tablespoon salt

Directions:

Combine your green beans and oil and stir well to coat. Season with salt and stir again.

Place the green beans on the racks of your Excalibur and set to 125F.

Dehydrate for 12 hours or until the beans are dehydrated and crispy.

Remove the green beans from the racks and store in a cool dry place.

Nutrition:

Calories: 130

Fat: 5 grams

Carbs: 20 grams

Protein: 2 grams

24. Sweet Potato Chips

Preparation Time: 15 minutes

Cooking Time: 14 hours

Servings: 6

Ingredients:

2 large sweet potatoes

2 teaspoons coconut oil, melted

2 teaspoons salt

Directions:

Slice the potatoes into thin rounds. Combine your potato slices, salt, and coconut oil and toss to coat.

Place ParaFlexx Screens on the racks of your Excalibur Food Dehydrator and place your potato on the screens in a single layer.

Set your Excalibur to 125F and dehydrate for 12 to 14 hours or until crisp. Transfer to a tray and store in a cool dry place if not using immediately.

Nutrition:

Calories: 125

Fat: 10 grams

Carbs: 9 grams

Protein: 1 gram

25. Dried Cilantro

Preparation Time: 10 minutes

Cooking Time: 3 hours 10 minutes

Servings: 12

Ingredients:

2 bunches fresh cilantro

Directions:

You can dehydrate your cilantro with or without the stems; it's totally up to you. Rinse and dry the cilantro and place it in a single layer on the racks of your Excalibur Food Dehydrator.

Set your Excalibur to 110F and dehydrate for 3 hours. Remove the dried cilantro from the racks and store in jars or zipper lock bags until ready to use.

Nutrition

Calories: 3.68

Fat: 0.083 grams

Carbs: 0.587 grams

Protein: 0.341 grams

26. Tomato Powder

Preparation Time: 10 minutes

Cooking Time: 4 hours 10 minutes

Servings: 24

Ingredients:

3 lbs. fresh tomatoes

Directions:

Slice the tomatoes about a 1/8 inch thick. Place ParaFlexx Screens on the racks of your Excalibur Food Dehydrator.

Lay the tomato slices on the screens in a single layer so they do not touch. Set your Excalibur Food Dehydrator to 150F and dehydrate for 4 hours.

When tomatoes are entirely dehydrated, transfer them to a blender, and pulse until a fine powder form. Store the powder in a jar or zipper lock bag.

Nutrition:

Calories: 86

Fat: 0.12 grams

Carbs: 21.17 grams

Protein: 3.66 grams

27. Plum Fruit Leather

Preparation Time: 30 minutes

Cooking Time: 8 hours 20 minutes

Servings: 12

Ingredients:

6 purple or red plums split and pitted

2 tablespoons lemon juice

2 teaspoons ground cinnamon

1/4 cup water

Directions:

Place the plums and water in a pot and simmer until the plums begin to break down, about 10 to 15 minutes.

When the plums are soft, pour into a blender and blend until smooth. Add the lemon juice and cinnamon and blend.

Place ParaFlexx Screens on the racks of your Excalibur and set to 140F.

Pour the puree onto the screens and use a spatula to spread the puree evenly, about 1/8 inch thick.

Dehydrate for 8 hours. Make sure the leather is entirely dehydrated and not sticky before removing from the screens.

Nutrition:

Calories: 31

Fat: 0 gram

Carbs: 7 grams

Protein: 0 gram

28. Strawberry Passion Fruit Leather

Preparation Time: 20 minutes

Cooking Time: 6 hours 10 minutes

Servings: 6

Ingredients:

2 cups fresh strawberries, stems removed

2 tablespoons passion fruit syrup

1 cup applesauce

Directions:

Place the strawberries, passion fruit syrup, and applesauce into a blender and puree until smooth.

Place ParaFlexx Screens on the racks of your Excalibur Food Dehydrator and pour the puree onto the screens.

Use a spatula to distribute the puree so it is about 1/8-inch think evenly.

Set your Excalibur to 140F and dehydrate for 6 hours.

Make sure your leather is wholly dehydrated and not sticky before removing from the screens.

Nutrition:

Calories: 45

Fat: 0 gram

Carbs: 12 grams

Protein: 0 gram

29. Citrus Potpourri

Preparation Time: 20 minutes

Cooking Time: 12 hours 15 minutes

Servings: 5

Ingredients:

2 lemons

2 oranges

6 cinnamon sticks

3 tablespoons dried cloves

Directions:

Slice the lemons and oranges between 1/8 and 1/4-inch-thick and place them on the racks of your Excalibur Food Dehydrator in a single layer so the slices are not touching.

Set your Excalibur to 150F and dehydrate for 12 hours. The citrus should be dry and firm to the touch and not sticky.

Remove the slices from the racks and divide among bowls or jars with equal amounts of cinnamon sticks and dried cloves.

Nutrition:

Calories: 190

Fat: 0 gram

Carbs: 41 grams

Protein: 7 grams

30. Dried Rose Petals

Preparation Time: 10 minutes

Cooking Time: 4 to 5 hours

Servings: 15

Ingredients:

Fresh rose petals, stems removed

Directions:

Select the type of rose you would like to use. Different varieties have different aromas, and some are stronger and sweeter than others.

For best results, only dehydrate one type of flower at a time because different types of roses require different drying times.

Remove the rose petals from the stems and place the petals on the rack of your Excalibur Food Dehydrator in single layers.

Set your Excalibur to 115F and dehydrate for 4 to 5 hours, or until the petals are dehydrated.

Your dried rose petals should retain their intense aromas for several months.

Nutrition:

Calories: 37

Fat: 0 gram

Carbs: 8 grams

Protein: 0 gram

Chapter 5: Tasty Recipes

31. Vegan Bread

Preparation Time: 30 minutes

Cooking Time: 6 hours

Servings: 6

Ingredients:

1 head cauliflower

1 teaspoon turmeric

2 tablespoons flax seed

1/2 cup psyllium hust

1/2 cup brewer's yeast

4 large zucchinis

Salt and black pepper

Directions:

Place cauliflower and zucchini in a food processor and pulse until they form a paste. Add the turmeric, flax seeds, psyllium, yeast, and a pinch of salt and black pepper. Pulse again until all ingredients are thoroughly combined. Place ParaFlexx Screens on the racks of your Excalibur Food Dehydrator. Form the mixture into slices about 1/2-inch-thick, and place on the screens. Set your Excalibur to 150F and dehydrate for 6 hours. The bread should not be dehydrated. One side should be slightly soft.

Nutrition:

Calories: 219

Fat: 1.9 grams

Carbs: 61.6 grams

Protein: 10.1 grams

32. Fluffy Dinner Rolls

Preparation Time: 15 minutes

Cooking Time: 7 hours

Servings: 6

Ingredients:

2 cups almond flour

1 cup psyllium

3 tablespoons ground flax seeds

1 tablespoon onion powder

2 teaspoons garlic powder

1 tablespoon lemon juice

1 teaspoon salt

1/3 cup water

Directions:

In a large bowl, combine the flour, psyllium, flax seeds, onion powder, garlic powder, lemon juice, salt, and water. Mix well until combined.

Form the mixture into 6 round rolls.

Place ParaFlexx Screens on the racks of your Excalibur. Place the rolls on the screens so they are not touching. Dehydrate at 145F for one hour, then lower the temperature to 110F for the remaining 6 hours. Remove from the screens and serve warm or allow to cool before storing.

Nutrition:

Calories: 319

Fat: 7.1 grams

Carbs: 95.2 grams

Protein: 3.5 grams

33. Herb and Almond Crackers

Preparation Time: 10 minutes

Cooking Time: 12 hours

Servings: 6

Ingredients:

2 cups almonds

1/2 cup ground flax seeds

1/4 cup brewer's yeast

3/4 cups water

2 tablespoons fresh rosemary, finely chopped

1 teaspoon salt

1/2 teaspoon black pepper

Directions:

In a food processor, combine the almonds, flax seed, yeast, salt, and pepper. Pulse until well combined.

Slowly add the water while continuing to pulse until a paste form.

Place ParaFlexx Screens on the racks of your Excalibur and spread a thin layer of the paste onto each screen. Set your Excalibur to 115F and dehydrate for 12 hours or until the crackers are crispy. Remove from the screens and break into small pieces to serve.

Nutrition:

Calories: 260

Fat: 19.3 grams

Carbs: 13.3 grams

Protein: 11.6 grams

34. Carrot Crackers

Preparation Time: 20 minutes

Cooking Time: 12 hours

Servings: 12

Ingredients:

6 large carrots, peeled

1/2 cup ground flax seeds

1 tomato, diced

Juice from 1 lemon

1/2 cup sesame seeds

1/2 cup chia seeds

3/4 cups water

Directions:

In a food processor, combine the carrots, flax seeds, tomato, lemon juice, and water, and pulse until a paste forms. Add the chia seeds, and sesame seeds and stir to combine.

Place ParaFlexx Screens on the racks of your Excalibur Food Dehydrator. Spread the paste evenly on the screens about 1/4 inch thick.

Set your Excalibur to 105F and dehydrate for 12 hours. Remove the crackers from the Excalibur and allow to cool completely. The crackers will become crispy as they cool.

Nutrition:

Calories: 122

Fat: 7.4 grams

Carbs: 10.8 grams

Protein: 3.9 grams

35. Nuts and Seeds Crackers

Preparation Time: 4 hours

Cooking Time: 24 hours

Servings: 20

Ingredients:

1 cup sunflower seeds

1 cup Brazil nuts

1 cup almonds

2 tablespoons tomato paste

1 cup red bell pepper, minced

1 cup ground flax seed

1 tablespoon salt

Directions:

In a bowl of water, soak the sunflower seeds, Brazil nuts, and almonds for 4 hours.

In a food processor, combine the sunflower seeds, Brazil nuts, almonds, tomato paste, bell pepper, flax seed, and salt. Pulse until the paste is smooth.

Place ParaFlexx Screens on the racks of your Excalibur. Pour the paste onto the screens and use a spatula to spread the mixture evenly about 1/8 inch thick.

Set your Excalibur to 115F and dehydrate for 24 hours.

Nutrition:

Calories: 113

Fat: 9.4 grams

Carbs: 4.6 grams

Protein: 3.5 grams

36. Greek Herb Blend

Preparation Time: 5 minutes

Cooking Time: 24 hours

Servings: 24

Ingredients:

1 bunch fresh basil

1 bunch fresh oregano

1 bunch fresh rosemary

1 bunch fresh thyme

1/2 onion, minced

3 cloves garlic, minced

Directions:

Wash and dry the fresh herbs and place a different herb on each rack of your Excalibur Food Dehydrator.

Place a ParaFlexx Screen on the remaining rack and place the onion on one side and the garlic on the other.

Set your Excalibur to 115F and dehydrate for 24 hours.

When the herbs, garlic, and onion are all dehydrated, transfer them to a blender and pulse until finely chopped and combined.

Nutrition:

Calories: 4

Fat: 0 gram

Carbs: 0.6 grams

Protein: 0.1 gram

37. Italian Herb Blend

Preparation Time: 10 minutes

Cooking Time: 24 hours

Servings: 24

Ingredients:

1 bunch fresh basil

1 bunch fresh oregano

1 bunch fresh rosemary

1 bunch fresh marjoram

1/2 bunch cilantro

1/2 bunch fresh thyme

Directions:

Wash all of the herbs and remove the leaves from the stems. In a large bowl, combine all of the herbs, and mix well.

Place the herb mix on the racks of your Excalibur Food Dehydrator and set to 115F. Dehydrate for 24 hours. Make sure all of the herbs are thoroughly dried before removing them from the dehydrator.

When herbs are dried, pour them into a blender, and pulse until the herbs are chopped and well mixed. Store in jars or zipper lock bags.

Nutrition:

Calories: 3

Fat: 0.1 gram

Carbs: 0.6 grams

Protein: 0.1 gram

38. Lemon Basil Blend

Preparation Time: 15 minutes

Cooking Time: 12 hours

Servings: 24

Ingredients:

2 bunches fresh basil

Juice from 1 lemon

Directions:

Rinse and dry your basil and remove the leaves from the stems.

Place the basil leaves in a large bowl and sprinkle the lemon juice over them. Mix well until all of the leaves are coated in lemon juice.

Place the basil in a single layer on the racks of your Excalibur Food Dehydrator. Try to keep the leaves from touching.

Set your Excalibur to 115F and dehydrate for 24 hours. When the basil is finished, they should feel dry and not sticky.

Remove the basil from the racks and store in jars or zipper lock bags until ready to use.

Nutrition:

Calories: 1

Fat: 0 gram

Carbs: 0.2 grams

Protein: 0 gram

39. Apple Cinnamon Potpourri

Preparation Time: 15 minutes

Cooking Time: 12 hours

Servings: 3

Ingredients:

2 red delicious apples

1 tablespoon ground cinnamon

Juice from 1 lemon

Directions:

Slice the apples into even slices around 1/8 inch thick. In a large bowl combine the apples and lemon juice. Stir well to make sure all of the apple slices are coated in lemon juice. Sprinkle in the cinnamon and stir again.

Place the apple slices on the racks of your Excalibur Food Dehydrator in a single layer so they are not touching.

Set your Excalibur to 150F and dehydrate for 12 hours. The apple slices should be thoroughly dried and no longer sticky. Remove from the racks and place around the house or store in airtight jars until ready to use.

Nutrition:

Calories: 120

Fat: 2 grams

Carbs: 24 grams

Protein: 2 grams

40. Citrus Potpourri

Preparation Time: 15 minutes

Cooking Time: 12 hours

Servings: 3

Ingredients:

2 lemons

2 oranges

6 cinnamon sticks

3 tablespoons dried cloves

Directions:

Slice the lemons and oranges between 1/8 and 1/4-inch-thick and place them on the racks of your Excalibur Food Dehydrator in a single layer so the slices are not touching.

Set your Excalibur to 150F and dehydrate for 12 hours. The citrus should be dry and firm to the touch and not sticky.

Remove the slices from the racks and divide among bowls or jars with equal amounts of cinnamon sticks and dried cloves.

Nutrition:

Calories: 35

Fat: 0 gram

Carbs: 9 grams

Protein: 0 gram

41. Lavender Potpourri

Preparation Time: 5 minutes

Cooking Time: 6 hours

Servings: 2

Ingredients:

Fresh lavender

Essential oils (optional)

Directions:

Collect lavender and trim them so there are several inches of stem below the flowers. Place the flowers on the racks of your Excalibur Food Dehydrator in a single layer. If using essential oils, sprinkle a few drops on the flowers before you start dehydrating.

Set your Excalibur to 115F and dehydrate for 6 hours. Remove the flowers from the racks and place around the house, or store in an airtight bag until ready to use.

Nutrition:

Calories: 70

Fat: 0 gram

Carbs: 17 grams

Protein: 0 gram

42. 3-Ingredient Banana Raisin Cookies

Preparation Time: 30 minutes

Cooking Time: 12 to 14 hours

Servings: 6

Ingredients:

1 very ripe banana, mashed

1 cup raisins

1 cup sweetened flake coconut

Directions:

Rehydrate raisins for 20 minutes in warm water.

Combine banana, raisins and coconut in a food processor until a paste form.

Dehydrate for 6-8 hours at 110 degrees. Flip mixture over and dehydrate for another 6 hours.

Nutrition:

Calories: 104

Fat: 4.1 grams

Carbs: 16.3 grams

Protein: 1.3 grams

43. Apple-Cherry-Apricot Fruit Leather

Preparation Time: 20 minutes

Cooking Time: 8 to 10 hours

Servings: 6

Ingredients:

1 cup peeled apricots, sliced into chunks

1 cup granny smith apples, peeled, cored and cut into small chunks

½ cup cherries, stems discarded and pitted

1-2 tablespoon honey

Directions:

Puree apricots, apples and cherries in a food processor. Add honey and pulse.

Pour mixture onto fruit leather sheets.

Set the temperature to 135 degrees.

Dry for 8-10 hours, or until leathery to touch.

Nutrition:

Calories: 42

Fat: 0.1 gram

Carbs: 10.8 grams

Protein: 0.2 grams

44. Apple Pie Leather

Preparation Time: 20 minutes

Cooking Time: 8 to 24 hours

Servings: 6

Ingredients:

6 apples, peeled, cored and chopped

1 cup coconut milk

2 cups applesauce

¼ cup honey

1 teaspoon ground cinnamon

1 teaspoon. apple pie spice

2 tablespoons. finely chopped raisins

Directions:

Place all the ingredients needed in a food processor and pulse once or twice.

Spread mixture on greased fruit leather dehydrator sheets.

Dehydrate for 8-24 hours at 135 degrees.

Cut into strips and roll into cylinders

Nutrition:

Calories: 20

Fat: 0.1 gram

Carbs: 5.4 grams

Protein: 0.1 gram

45. Asian Pear and Ginger Treats

Preparation Time: 20 minutes

Cooking Time: 9 to 12 hours

Servings: 6 to 8

Ingredients:

6 medium sized Asian pears, peeled, pitted and cored

1 ½ teaspoon honey

4 tablespoon warm water

1 small knob of ginger, finely grated

Directions:

In a bowl, mix honey and ginger. Add the water and mix well.

Slice Asian pears into uniform slices, around ¼ inch thick. Arrange pear slices onto dehydrator tray and brush with a thin layer of ginger-honey mixture.

Dehydrate for 9-12 hours at 135 degrees.

Nutrition:

Calories: 18

Fat: 0 gram

Carbs: 4.9 grams

Protein: 0.1 gram

46. Banana Cocoa Leather

Preparation Time: 30 minutes

Cooking Time: 8 to 10 hours

Servings: 6

Ingredients:

4 bananas

2 tablespoons cocoa powder

1-2 tablespoons. corn syrup

1 teaspoon lemon juice

Directions:

Puree all ingredients until smooth.

Pour mixture onto dehydrator trays and spread to ¼ inch thickness. Dehydrate at 130 degree for 8-10 hours. About half way through, flip leather to the other side.

Nutrition:

Calories: 42

Fat: 0.8 grams

Carbs: 11 grams

Protein: 1.1 gram

47. Cherry Coconut Almond Cookies

Preparation Time: 1 hour 20 minutes

Cooking Time: 6 hours

Servings: 8

Ingredients:

1 cup salted almond butter

1 cup pitted dates (soaked in the water for ½ hour)

1 cup dried cherries (soaked in the water for ½ hour)

1 cup crushed almonds

1/8- 1/4 cup water

1 cup shredded coconut

Directions:

In a food processor, pulse the dried fruits. Add almond butter and crushed almonds. Pulse again.

Add in water slowly until the dough can be rolled into balls. Do not allow dough to get too runny. Flatten balls into discs and dip into shredded coconut to adhere to both sides.

Place on dehydrator sheet and set temperature to 145 degrees. Dehydrate for 3 hours and then flip over to other side for 3 hours.

Nutrition:

Calories: 151

Fat: 12.6 grams

Carbs: 6.6 grams

Protein: 4.6 grams

48. Chewy Lemony Treats

Preparation Time: 20 minutes

Cooking Time: 8 hours

Servings: 6 to 8

Ingredients:

2 cups almonds

2 cups unsweetened coconut flakes

6 tablespoons lemon juice

1 teaspoon vanilla extract

Dash of cinnamon

¼ cup maple syrup

Directions:

Place all the almonds in the food processor and pulse until a flour-like consistency develops.

Add coconut and process with the ground nuts. Add the lemon juice, (zest if using), vanilla extract, cinnamon and maple syrup.

Scoop out batter into mini-balls and flatten. Place on dehydrator sheets and dehydrate for 8 hours at 115 degrees for a chewy texture.

Nutrition:

Calories: 185

Fat: 16.1 grams

Carbs: 7 grams

Protein: 4.1 grams

49. Energy Balls

Preparation Time: 30 minutes

Cooking Time: 3 hours

Servings: 6

Ingredients:

1 ½ cup raw cashews, soaked

2 cups dates, soaked

½ cup raisins

5 tablespoons unsweetened cocoa powder

2 tablespoons maple syrup

½ teaspoon vanilla extract

½ teaspoon salt

½ cup crushed cashews

½ cup unsweetened coconut flakes

Directions:

Remove cashews and dates from soaking water. Place them in a food processor and pulse. Add the raisins, cocoa powder, maple syrup, vanilla extract and salt and blend until it reaches a paste-like consistency.

Once the mixture feels like a dough, roll into balls. Mix crushed cashews and coconut flakes in a small bowl and roll the balls in the mixture.

Place balls on dehydrator trays and dry at 135 degrees for 3 hours.

Nutrition:

Calories: 125

Fat: 8.9 grams

Carbs: 11.1 grams

Protein: 3.1 grams

50. Fruit Sprinkles

Preparation Time: 20 minutes

Cooking Time: 6 to 8 hours

Servings: 6 to 8

Ingredients:

1 cup raspberries or strawberries, hulled

1 tablespoon sugar

1 tablespoon orange juice

Zest of 2 lemons

Zest of 2 oranges

Directions:

Dice strawberries and raspberries into small pieces.

Combine with sugar, juice and lemon and orange zest.

Spread mixture on dehydrator sheets.

Dehydrate for 6-8 hours at 118 degrees. At this point, fruit should be thoroughly dried.

Place all the mixture in a spice grinder and pulse several times until you have sprinkles. Top your favorite treats with fruit sprinkles for added flavor and color.

Nutrition:

Calories: 25

Fat: 0 gram

Carbs: 6.5 grams

Protein: 0.1 gram

51. Goji Berry Leather

Preparation Time: 1 hour 15 minutes

Cooking Time: 7 hours

Servings: 2

Ingredients:

1 cup dried goji berries

2 cups unsweetened applesauce

2 tablespoons honey

Directions:

Place goji berries in 1 cup of water and let soak until they are rehydrated, about 1 hour.

Pour berries, soaking water, applesauce and honey into the blender and blend until smooth. Add more water if necessary.

Spread onto dehydrator sheets and dry at 135 degrees for 6-7 hours.

Nutrition:

Calories: 64

Fat: 0.8 grams

Carbs: 14 grams

Protein: 0.5 grams

52. Honey Banana Walnut Chips

Preparation Time: 20 minutes

Cooking Time: 8 to 12 hours

Servings: 1

Ingredients:

4 bananas, peeled and cut into ¼ pieces

¼ cup honey, diluted slightly with water

½ cup crushed walnuts

Directions:

Dip banana slices into diluted honey. Sprinkle with crushed walnuts.

Place bananas on dehydrator trays and dry at 135 degrees for 2 hours. Then set the temperature at 115 degrees and dehydrate for another 6-12 hours.

Nutrition:

Calories: 136

Fat: 8.2 grams

Carbs: 15 grams

Protein: 3.8 grams

53. Nothing But Fruit Bars

Preparation Time: 30 minutes

Cooking Time: 18 hours

Servings: 8

Ingredients:

2 cups sprouted buckwheat or quinoa

1 cup dates

1 cup dried apricots

1 tablespoon cinnamon

1/8 teaspoon cardamom

1 pear or apple, peeled, cored and diced

Directions:

Place all ingredients in a blender. Blend until smooth.

Spread the mixture onto dehydrator trays. Use a spatula to smooth. Dehydrate for 18 hours at 130 degrees.

Nutrition:

Calories: 98

Fat: 1.6 grams

Carbs: 17.6 grams

Protein: 3.6 grams

54. Peanut Butter, Banana and Graham Cracker Cookie Bars

Preparation Time: 20 minutes

Cooking Time: 14 hours

Servings: 8

Ingredients:

3 ripe bananas, sliced

½ cup peanut butter

½ cup oats

2 cups graham cracker cookies, crushed

½ cup cacao nibs

Directions:

In a bowl, mash the bananas with the peanut butter.

Mix the oats, graham cracker crumbs, and cacao nibs. Blend with banana and peanut butter mixture.

Gather into a ball and shape into a rectangle using waxed paper or a buttered spatula.

Chill for 8 hours or overnight, preferably.

When you remove chilled dough, slice into ¼ inch slices and dehydrate at 135-145 degrees for 6 hours. The texture of these bars will be more like a cookie and less like a cracker.

Nutrition:

Calories: 119

Fat: 4.8 grams

Carbs: 16.7 grams

Protein: 2.7 grams

55. Raspberry Banana Fruit Leather

Preparation Time: 30 minutes

Cooking Time: 8 to 10 hours

Servings: 24

Ingredients:

1 banana

1 cup raspberries

2 tablespoon raspberry jam

1 teaspoon lemon juice

Directions:

Puree banana, raspberries, jam and lemon juice until smooth.

Spread mixture evenly, about 1/8-inch-thick, onto fruit leather sheets.

Set the temperature to 135 degrees. Dry for 8-10 hours, or until leathery to touch.

Nutrition:

Calories: 36

Fat: 0.1 gram

Carbs: 9 grams

Protein: 0.3 grams

56. Spiced Apple Chips

Preparation Time: 30 minutes

Cooking Time: 6 to 8 hours

Servings: 12

Ingredients:

3-4 ripe apples (any variety)

1 tablespoon ground cinnamon

1/8 teaspoon. either nutmeg, cloves, allspice, ginger or cardamom

1 tablespoon sugar

Directions:

Slice the apple into thin rounds, between 1/8 – 1/4 inch thick. Peels can be removed or left intact. Remove core and seeds.

Toss sliced apples with the cinnamon, nutmeg, cloves and sugar.

Arrange in a single line in your dehydrator and set temperature to 135. Allow apples to dehydrate for 6-8 hours.

Nutrition:

Calories: 36

Fat: 0.1 gram

Carbs: 10.3 grams

Protein: 0.2 grams

57. Candied Pineapple Slices

Preparation Time: 40 minutes

Cooking Time: 16 hours

Servings: 24

Ingredients:

1 large ripe pineapple

2 cups water

1 cup light corn syrup

1 cup granulated sugar

Directions:

Choose a ripe, unbruised pineapple then remove the skin and core.

Cut the pineapple into strips about ½-inch thick.

Whisk together the water, corn syrup and sugar in a medium saucepan equipped with a stainless-steel blanching basket.

Bring the mixture to a boil then add the prepared fruit.

Reduce the heat and simmer for 5 to 10 minutes then drain the pineapple.

Rinse the pineapple in lukewarm water then spread the slices in a single layer on your dehydrator trays.

Dehydrate the pineapple for 12 to 16 hours at a temperature of 135°F (57°C) – turn the slices after 8 hours to make sure they dry evenly.

When the pineapple slices are firm and chewy, cool them then store in an airtight plastic or glass container in a cool, dry location.

Nutrition:

Calories: 93

Fat: 0 gram

Carbs: 23 grams

Protein: 0 gram

58. Candied Ginger

Preparation Time: 20 minutes

Cooking Time: 4 hours

Servings: 6 to 8

Ingredients:

Fresh ginger roots

Water, as needed

Granulated sugar, as needed

Directions:

Peel the ginger then cut into thin slices or chunks.

Place the ginger in a medium saucepan and pour in enough water to cover it.

Add an equal amount of sugar then bring to a boil.

Reduce the heat and simmer for about 45 minutes, then drain off the syrup, reserving it.

Measure out the ginger then add it back to the saucepan.

Add an equal amount of sugar along with two tablespoons of the reserved syrup for every cup of prepared ginger.

Bring the ginger to boil over medium heat then reduce heat slightly and simmer until all of the liquid cooks off.

Stir the ginger frequently, boiling it until the sugar separates and dries.

Remove the pan from the heat then spread the ginger slices on your dehydrator trays. Let the ginger cool then store in glass jars, sealed tightly with the lids.

Nutrition:

Calories: 8

Fat: 0 gram

Carbs: 2 grams

Protein: 0 gram

59. Soy Marinated Salmon Jerky

Preparation Time: 40 minutes

Cooking Time: 16 hours

Servings: 12

Ingredients:

1 lbs. boneless salmon fillet

Salt and pepper to taste

½ cup apple cider vinegar

2 tablespoons low-sodium soy sauce

1 tablespoon fresh lemon juice

2 teaspoons paprika

½ teaspoon garlic powder

Directions:

Freeze the salmon for about 30 minutes until it is firm. Meanwhile, whisk together the apple cider vinegar, soy sauce, and lemon juice in a mixing bowl. Add the paprika and garlic powder then stir well. Season the salmon with salt and pepper to taste then remove the skin. Slice the salmon into ¼-inch thick strips then place them in a bowl or glass dish. Pour in the marinade, turning to coat, then cover with plastic and chill for 12 hours. Drain the salmon slices and place them on paper towels to soak up the extra liquid. Spread the salmon slices on your dehydrator trays in a single layer. Dry for 3 to 4 hours at 145°F (63°C) until it is dried but still tender and chewy. Cool the salmon jerky completely then store in airtight containers in a cool, dark location.

Nutrition:

Calories: 40

Fat: 1 gram

Carbs: 5 grams

Protein: 4 grams

60. Dehydrated Maple Oat Granola

Preparation Time: 30 minutes

Cooking Time: 5 to 6 hours

Servings: 6 to 8

Ingredients:

2 cups old-fashioned oats

½ cup raw walnuts, coarsely chopped

½ cup dried cherries, chopped

¼ cup raw sunflower seeds

3 tablespoons pure maple syrup

2 tablespoons coconut oil

½ teaspoon almond extract

¼ teaspoon salt

Directions:

Combine all of the ingredients in a large mixing bowl and stir until well combined.

Spread the mixture onto your dehydrator trays as evenly as possible.

Dehydrate at 115°F (46°C) for about 5 to 6 hours until dried and crunchy.

Cool the granola then break it into chunks and store in a glass jar.

Nutrition:

Calories: 94

Fat: 3 grams

Carbs: 12 grams

Protein: 10 grams

Chapter 6: Easy Recipes

61. Pickle Chips

Preparation Time: 5 minutes

Cooking Time: 12 hours

Servings: 12

Ingredients:

1 jar large dill pickles

Directions:

Remove pickles from the jar and pat dry with paper towels. Slice the pickles length-wise into long, thin slabs about 1/4 inch thick.

Lay the pickle slices on the racks of your Nesco Snack Master and set to 125F. Dehydrate for 12 hours or until the pickles are completely dried.

Remove from the racks and eat like chips or store and rehydrate when needed. To rehydrate simply place the dried pickle slices in a bowl of lukewarm water and wait 5 to 10 minutes.

Nutrition:

Calories: 1

Fat: 0 gram

Carbs: 0.3 grams

Protein: 0.1 gram

62. Beet Chips

Preparation Time: 12 hours

Cooking Time: 12 hours

Servings: 10

Ingredients:

4 large beets sliced into thin rounds

1 cup apple cider vinegar

Directions:

In a wide shallow bowl or tray, pour the vinegar and arrange the beet slices in a single layer. Allow the beet slices to soak for 12 hours.

Remove the beets from the vinegar and pat dry with paper towels.

Lay the beet slices on the racks of your Nesco SnackMaster and set to 125F. Dehydrate for 12 hours or until beet slices are completely dried. Store in zip-lock bags until ready to use.

Nutrition:

Calories: 23

Fat: 0.1 gram

Carbs: 4.2 grams

Protein: 0.7 grams

63. Potato Chips

Preparation Time: 10 minutes

Cooking Time: 6 hours

Servings: 6

Ingredients:

2 russet potatoes, peeled

Vegetable oil spray

Salt

Directions:

Rinse and peel the potatoes and use a mandolin to slice them into thin rounds. Lay the rounds on a baking sheet and spray with cooking oil on both sides.

Sprinkle the rounds with salt and place on the racks of your SnackMaster. Set to 110F and dehydrate for 6 hours or until the chips are dried and crispy.

Store in a large zip-lock bag until ready to use.

Nutrition:

Calories: 49

Fat: 0.1 gram

Carbs: 11.2 grams

Protein: 1.2 grams

64. Dehydrated Coconut Wrap

Preparation Time: 15 minutes

Cooking Time: 16 hours

Servings: 1 to 2

Ingredients:

1 – 2 tablespoons of raw coconut water

2 cups raw coconut meat

1/2 teaspoon unrefined sea salt

Directions:

Put the coconut meat in a grinder or food processor and pulse to a mushy consistency.

Now add the salt and then alternate the pulsing with small quantities of coconut water until the mixture becomes spreadable in consistency but not too thin.

Spread the mixture to about 1/4-inch thickness on the dehydrator sheet and dry at 105 degrees. When it dries up on the top, flip it and dry the other side for a few hours.

Nutrition:

Calories: 70

Fat: 5 grams

Carbs: 6 grams

Protein: 1 gram

65. Dehydrated Banana Chips

Preparation Time: 10 minutes

Cooking Time: 20 hours

Servings: 6

Ingredients:

2 – 4 ripe bananas

Directions:

Cut the bananas into 1/8-inch-thick slices.

Prepare the dehydrator as per manufacturer's instructions and line it with parchment paper.

Spread out the banana slices on the parchment paper and dry them for 18 – 20 hours or until they are completely dry.

Nutrition:

Calories: 60

Fat: 0 gram

Carbs: 15 grams

Protein: 1 gram

66. Dehydrated Banana Candy

Preparation Time: 10 minutes

Cooking Time: 15 hours

Servings: 6

Ingredients:

2 – 4 ripe bananas

Directions:

Cut the bananas into 1/4-inch-thick slices.

Prepare the dehydrator as per manufacturer's instructions and line it with parchment paper.

Spread out the banana slices on the parchment paper and dry them for 15 hours.

Nutrition:

Calories: 14

Fat: 0 gram

Carbs: 3 grams

Protein: 0 gram

67. Garlic Jerky

Preparation Time: 15 minutes

Cooking Time: 4 hours

Servings: 8

Ingredients:

3 lbs. flank steak, cut into ¼ inch thick slices

2 tablespoon garlic powder

¼ cup coconut amino

Directions:

In a bowl, mix together garlic powder and coconut amino.

Add meat slices to the bowl and mix until well coated. Cover bowl and place in refrigerator for overnight.

Remove marinated meat slices from marinade and arrange meat slices on dehydrator racks.

Arrange dehydrator tray according to the manufacturer's instructions and dehydrate at 145 F/ 63 C for 4 hours.

Nutrition:

Calories: 344

Fat: 14.2 grams

Carbs: 3 grams

Protein: 47.7 grams

68. Sweet & Tangy Mango Slices

Preparation Time: 15 minutes

Cooking Time: 12 hours

Servings: 6

Ingredients:

4 mangoes

1 tablespoon honey

¼ cup lemon juice

Directions:

In a bowl, mix together lemon juice and honey and set aside.

Peel the mangoes and cut into ¼ inch thick slices.

Add mango slices in lemon honey mixture and coat well.

Arrange mango slices on dehydrator racks and dehydrate at 135 F/ 58 C for 12 hours.

Nutrition:

Calories: 147

Fat: 0.9 grams

Carbs: 36.7 grams

Protein: 1.9 grams

69. Dehydrated Bananas

Preparation Time: 15 minutes

Cooking Time: 8 hours

Servings: 4

Ingredients:

2 bananas, cut into 1/8-inch-thick slices

½ cup fresh lemon juice

Directions:

Add sliced bananas and lemon juice in a bowl and toss well.

Arrange sliced bananas on dehydrator racks and dehydrate at 135 F/ 58 C for 6-8 hours.

Nutrition:

Calories: 60

Fat: 0.4 grams

Carbs: 14.1 grams

Protein: 0.9 grams

70. Canned Peaches

Preparation Time: 10 minutes

Cooking Time: 8 hours

Servings: 4

Ingredients:

2 canned peaches

Directions:

Arrange peach slices on dehydrator racks and dehydrate at 135 F/ 58 C for 4 hours.

Turn peach slices to other side and dehydrate for 4 hours more.

Store in air-tight container.

Nutrition:

Calories: 30

Fat: 0.2 grams

Carbs: 7 grams

Protein: 0.7 grams

71. Peach Wedges

Preparation Time: 15 minutes

Cooking Time: 8 hours

Servings: 4

Ingredients:

3 peaches, cut and remove pits and sliced

½ cup lemon juice

Directions:

Add lemon juice and peach slices into the bowl and toss well.

Arrange peach slices on dehydrator racks and dehydrate at 135 F/ 58 C for 6-8 hours.

Nutrition:

Calories: 52

Fat: 0.5 grams

Carbs: 11.1 grams

Protein: 1.3 grams

72. Cinnamon Apple Chips

Preparation Time: 15 minutes

Cooking Time: 12 hours

Servings: 4

Ingredients:

4 apples, cored, sliced 1/8 inch thick

1 teaspoon ground cinnamon

2 cups water

1 tablespoon lemon juice

1 tablespoon vinegar

Directions:

In a bowl, add water, lemon juice, and vinegar and mix well.

Add apple slices in the water and let sit for 5 minutes.

Remove apple slices from water and pat dry with paper towel.

Arrange apple slices on a dehydrator tray and sprinkle with cinnamon and dehydrate at 135 F/ 58 C for 12 hours.

Nutrition:

Calories: 119

Fat: 0.4 grams

Carbs: 31.4 grams

Protein: 0.7 grams

73. Green Apple Chips

Preparation Time: 10 minutes

Cooking Time: 8 hours

Servings: 4

Ingredients:

4 green apples, cored and sliced 1/8 inch thick

½ lime juice

Directions:

Add apple slices and lime juice in a bowl and toss well and set aside for 5 minutes.

Arrange apple slices on dehydrator trays and dehydrate at 145 F/ 63 C for 8 hours.

Store in air-tight container.

Nutrition:

Calories: 117

Fat: 0.4 grams

Carbs: 31.3 grams

Protein: 0.6 grams

74. Sliced Strawberries

Preparation Time: 10 minutes

Cooking Time: 12 hours

Servings: 4

Ingredients:

2 cups strawberries, sliced ¼ inch thick

Directions:

Arrange strawberry slices on dehydrator trays and dehydrate at 135 F/ 58 C for 8-12 hours.

Store dried strawberries in air-tight container.

Nutrition:

Calories: 23

Fat: 0.2 grams

Carbs: 5.5 grams

Protein: 0.5 grams

75. Dried Raspberries

Preparation Time: 10 minutes

Cooking Time: 18 hours

Servings: 4

Ingredients:

4 cups raspberries, wash and dry

¼ cup lemon juice

Directions:

Add raspberries and lemon juice in a bowl and toss well.

Arrange raspberries on dehydrator trays and dehydrate at 135 F/58 C for 15-18 hours.

Store in air-tight container.

Nutrition:

Calories: 68

Fat: 0.9 grams

Carbs: 15 grams

Protein: 1.6 grams

76. Dried Kiwi

Preparation Time: 10 minutes

Cooking Time: 12 hours

Servings: 4

Ingredients:

4 kiwis, peeled and cut into ¼ inch thick slices

Directions:

Arrange kiwi slices on dehydrator trays and dehydrate at 135 F/ 58 C for 6-12 hours or until kiwi slices completely dry.

Store in air-tight container.

Nutrition:

Calories: 46

Fat: 0.4 grams

Carbs: 11.1 grams

Protein: 0.9 grams

77. Dehydrated Figs

Preparation Time: 15 minutes

Cooking Time: 8 to 24 hours

Servings: 6

Ingredients:

2 lbs. Fresh Ripe Figs

Directions:

Fill a large pot with water and bring it to the boil. Add the figs, blanch them for half a minute, take them out and immediately place in a pot filled with ice cold water.

Arrange the figs on your dehydrator trays and dehydrate at 135F / 57C for 8-24 hours depending on the size of the figs.

When the figs are dry but still chewy, remove them from the dehydrator, allow to cool and store in airtight containers.

Nutrition:

Calories: 111.0

Fat: 0.5 grams

Carbs: 28.8 grams

Protein: 1.1 gram

78. Dehydrated Clementine

Preparation Time: 10 minutes

Cooking Time: 12 to 14 hours

Servings: 4

Ingredients:

10 Clementine

Directions:

1. Rinse the clementine (do not peel them) and slice into thin slices. Arrange on your dehydrator trays and dehydrate at 135F / 57C for 12-14 hours, depending on the thickness of the slices.

2. Allow to cool and store in airtight containers.

Nutrition:

Calories: 87.5

Fat: 0.0 gram

Carbs: 22.5 grams

Protein: 2.5 grams

79. Dried Watermelon

Preparation Time: 15 minutes

Cooking Time: 11 hours

Servings: 8

Ingredients:

1 Watermelon, medium-sized

Sea Salt, to taste

Directions:

Chop the watermelon into wedges and cut them into ¼-inch pieces.

Place in a bowl, sprinkle with salt and toss to coat.

Arrange the slices on dehydrator trays and dehydrate at 140F / 60C for about 11 hours or until the desired doneness.

Allow to cool and store in airtight containers.

Nutrition:

Calories: 168.7

Fat: 0.7 grams

Carbs: 42.6 grams

Protein: 3.4 grams

80. Camping Egg Breakfast

Preparation Time: 20 minutes

Cooking Time: 8 to 10 hours

Servings: 5

Ingredients:

5 eggs, large

Directions:

Crack the eggs in a bowl. You may need to split the amount for the size of your dehydrator trays.

Whisk eggs well, till blended fully and a bit foamy.

Carefully pour eggs into fruit leather dehydrator tray.

Dehydrate the eggs at 140F for 8 – 10 hours till flaky and fully dried. The egg flakes will be oily, so it should be easy to scrape them away without them sticking to tray when they have fully dried. If your eggs still feel sticky, leave sticky eggs in dehydrator for a short additional time period.

Transfer the dried egg flakes to zipper top plastic bag. Place in the freezer for 1/2 to 1 full hour.

Remove the eggs from the freezer. Blend in your food processor till fully powdered. They should not stick to food processor sides at all. If they do, they need to dry more. Put eggs in dehydrator again if they need more drying.

Store the eggs in a zipper lock plastic bag in a freezer till ready for use.

Nutrition:

Calories: 40

Fat: 3 grams

Carbs: 1 gram

Protein: 3 grams

81. Pumpkin Lovers' Pancakes

Preparation Time: 10 minutes

Cooking Time: 15 minutes

Servings: 1

Ingredients:

3 & 1/2 ounces of batter mix, pancake

2 tablespoons of pumpkin powder

To fry: ghee (clarified butter)

Directions:

Combine the mixture of pancake batter with pumpkin powder in zipper top plastic bag.

Pack the ghee separately. Store till ready to use.

Nutrition:

Calories: 70

Fat: 3 grams

Carbs: 16 grams

Protein: 3 grams

82. Barley – Beef Stew

Preparation Time: 10 minutes

Cooking Time: 15 minutes

Servings: 1

Ingredients:

1/4 cup of ground beef, dehydrated

1/3 cup of cooked barley, dehydrated

1 tablespoon of carrots, dehydrated

1 tablespoon of green beans, dehydrated

1 teaspoon of celery, dehydrated

1 tablespoon of powdered tomato sauce

1 teaspoon of thyme, dried

1 teaspoon of bouillon powder, low sodium

Directions:

Mix all ingredients in med. zipper top bag.

Store till ready to use.

Nutrition:

Calories: 250

Fat: 4 grams

Carbs: 32 grams

Protein: 19 grams

83. Salmon & Cheese Pasta

Preparation Time: 10 minutes

Cooking Time: 10 minutes

Servings: 1

Ingredients:

1 tablespoon of milk powder, full cream

2 tablespoon of powdered cheddar cheese, freeze-dried

1 teaspoon of flour, all-purpose

2/3 cup of pre-cooked pasta, dehydrated

Salt, as desired

1 tablespoon of ghee (clarified butter)

1 x 2- & 1/2-ounce pouch of salmon, smoked

Directions:

Mix the flour, milk powder and cheese in small zipper top plastic bag.

Pack remainder of ingredients separately. Store till ready to use.

Nutrition:

Calories: 205

Fat: 8 grams

Carbs: 23 grams

Protein: 11 grams

84. Easy Seafood Curry

Preparation Time: 10 minutes

Cooking Time: 10 minutes

Servings: 1

Ingredients:

1/4 cup of basmati rice, cooked, dehydrated

1/4 cup of seafood mix, dehydrated

1 teaspoon. of curry paste, Thai yellow, dehydrated

2 tablespoon of powdered tomato sauce

3 tablespoon of powdered coconut milk

Directions:

Mix all ingredients in zipper top storage bag. Store till ready to serve.

Nutrition:

Calories: 169

Fat: 11 grams

Carbs: 9 grams

Protein: 9 grams

85. Chocolate & Almonds Breakfast Smoothie

Preparation Time: 30 minutes

Cooking Time: 6 to 12 hours

Servings: 1

Ingredients:

2 tablespoons of rolled oats or wheat berries

1 banana, whole

1 tablespoon of peanut butter or almond butter

1 teaspoon of flax seed, ground

1 teaspoon of powdered cocoa

3/4 cup of milk, almond

Directions:

Combine all ingredients in food processor.

Process on high speed setting till frothy and smooth.

Spread on a dehydrator tray covered with parchment paper or non-stick sheet.

Dehydrate at 115 degrees F for six to 12 hours, till fully brittle and dry.

Remove from the dehydrator. Allow to cool.

Grind the dried smoothie mixture into fine powder in coffee grinder.

Pack recipe in small sized zipper top plastic bag. Store till ready to use.

Nutrition:

Calories: 210

Fat: 14 grams

Carbs: 18 grams

Protein: 3 grams

86. Sausage Breakfast Scramble

Preparation Time: 10 minutes

Cooking Time: 10 minutes

Servings: 2

Ingredients:

4 tablespoons of pork sausage crumbs, freeze dried

4 tablespoons of crystal egg, whole

6 tomatoes, sun-dried

1 tablespoons of powdered tomato sauce

1/2 teaspoon of oregano, dried

2 tablespoons of Parmesan cheese, grated, freeze-dried

1 tablespoon of ghee (clarified butter)

Directions:

Mix the sausage crumbs, powdered eggs, oregano, powdered tomato sauce and sun-dried tomatoes in medium zipper top plastic bag.

Pack remainder of the ingredients separately. Store till ready to use.

Nutrition:

Calories: 272

Fat: 20 grams

Carbs: 4 grams

Protein: 22 grams

87. Italian Frittata

Preparation Time: 10 minutes

Cooking Time: 10 minutes

Servings: 1

Ingredients:

6 tablespoons of whole eggs, powdered

1 tablespoon of milk powder, full cream

2 tablespoons of chopped tomatoes, sun-dried

1/4 teaspoon of oregano, dried

1/4 teaspoon of marjoram, dried

Salt, sea and Pepper, ground

1 tablespoon of oil, olive

1 shallot

3/4 ounce of chorizo

1 tablespoon of Parmesan cheese, grated, freeze-dried

Directions:

Mix the dried herbs, tomatoes, milk and powdered eggs in zipper top plastic bag.

Pack remaining ingredients separately. Store till ready to use.

Nutrition:

Calories: 234

Fat: 18 grams

Carbs: 6 grams

Protein: 14 grams

88. Chili Mac

Preparation Time: 10 minutes

Cooking Time: 10 minutes

Servings: 1

Ingredients:

1/4 cup of ground beef, dehydrated

2/3 cup of pasta, dehydrated, pre-cooked

1/4 cup of canned beans, dehydrated

2 tablespoon of powdered tomato sauce

1 pinch of chili powder

1 handful of Parmesan or cheddar cheese, grated

Directions:

Mix the ground beef, pasta, chili, dried beans and powdered tomato sauce in medium zipper top plastic bag.

Pack the cheese separately.

Store till ready to use.

Nutrition:

Calories: 190

Fat: 2 grams

Carbs: 32 grams

Protein: 12 grams

89. Vegetable Pulp Pizza

Preparation Time: 10 minutes

Cooking Time: 15 hours

Servings: 8

Ingredients:

16 ounces of vegetable pulp

1 & 1/4 cup of flax meal

1 cup of water, filtered

2 tablespoons of tamari

1/4 teaspoon of salt, sea

3 cloves of garlic

1 jalapeno pepper

1 bell pepper, yellow

1/2 cup of yeast, nutritional

1 fresh lemon, juice only

Directions:

Blend together all the ingredients with the exception of sesame seeds.

After mixture is well mixed and creamy, sprinkle the seeds around the crust.

Spread on a dehydrator sheet. Dehydrate at 115F for 15 hours or longer. Store till you are ready to use.

Nutrition:

Calories: 180

Fat: 6 grams

Carbs: 23 grams

Protein: 26 grams

90. Irish Stew

Preparation Time: 10 minutes

Cooking Time: 15 minutes

Servings: 1

Ingredients:

1/4 cup of potatoes, dehydrated

1/4 cup of canned beef, dehydrated

2 teaspoons of carrots, dehydrated

1 tablespoon of green beans, dehydrated

1 tablespoon of fried onions, dehydrated

1 tablespoon of powdered beef gravy

1 teaspoon of thyme, dried

1 teaspoon of bouillon powder, low-sodium

Directions:

Mix all ingredients in medium zipper top plastic bag.

Store till ready to use.

Nutrition:

Calories: 486

Fat: 11 grams

Carbs: 36 grams

Protein: 25 grams

Chapter 7: Chapter 10: Medium Recipes

91. Dehydrated Crackers

Preparation Time: 20 minutes

Cooking Time: 12 hours

Servings: 12

Ingredients:

2 cups ground flaxseed

1 cup whole flaxseed

1 cup raw sunflower seeds

½ cup raw sesame seeds

2 2/3 cups water

1 teaspoon dried Italian seasoning

1 teaspoon salt

Directions:

Combine all of the ingredients in a large mixing bowl. Stir until thoroughly combined then spread the mixture on dehydrator sheets lined with parchment. Dry the mixture at 120°F (49°C) for 1 hour then reduce heat to 105°F (40.5°C). Let the crackers dry until they start to harden (about 4 hours) then use a sharp knife to score the mixture into square crackers. Continue drying the cracker mixture for another 8 hours or so until they hold their shape. Break the crackers apart along the scored line then place them on unlined dehydrator trays. Continue to dry for another few hours until the crackers are completely dry. Cool the crackers completely then store in airtight containers.

Nutrition:

Calories: 55.38

Fat: 5.12 grams

Carbs: 3.1 grams

Protein: 2.38 grams

92. Dried Vanilla Spiced Granola

Preparation Time: 30 minutes

Cooking Time: 18 to 20 hours

Servings: 16

Ingredients:

2 cups whole almonds, raw

1 ½ cups walnut halves, raw

½ cup raw pumpkin seeds

8 pitted Medjool dates

2 tablespoons raw honey

1 teaspoon vanilla extract

½ teaspoon ground cinnamon

¼ teaspoon ground nutmeg

Directions:

Place the almonds, walnuts, and pumpkin seeds in separate bowls. Cover with water and soak for 6 hours then drain completely. Soak the dates in water for 15 minutes just before using. Combine the dates, honey, vanilla extract, cinnamon and nutmeg in a food processor. Blend the ingredients into a paste then transfer to a bowl. Combine the soaked nuts and seeds in the food processor and pulse to chop. Stir the chopped nut mixture into the blended date mixture until well combined. Spread the mixture onto your dehydrator trays as evenly as possible. Dehydrate at 115°F (46°C) for about 18 to 20 hours until dried and crunchy. Break the granola into chunks and store in a glass jar.

Nutrition:

Calories: 140

Fat: 6 grams

Carbs: 21 grams

Protein: 4 grams

93. Teriyaki Beef Jerky

Preparation Time: 30 minutes

Cooking Time: 4 hours

Servings: 8

Ingredients:

2 ½ to 3 lbs. boneless beef sirloin

Salt and pepper to taste

¼ cup low-sodium soy sauce

¼ cup light brown sugar, packed

2 tablespoons liquid smoke

1 teaspoon cider vinegar

Directions:

Whisk together the soy sauce, sugar, liquid smoke and cider vinegar in a mixing bowl.

Trim the fat from the beef and cut it into ¼-inch thick strips.

Season the beef with salt and pepper to taste then add to the bowl with the marinade.

Toss to coat then cover with plastic and chill for 24 hours.

Spread the meat slices on your dehydrator trays in a single layer.

Dry for 4 hours at 145°F (63°C) until it is dried but still tender and chewy.

Cool the jerky completely then store in airtight containers in a cool, dark location.

Nutrition:

Calories: 84

Fat: 2 grams

Carbs: 5 grams

Protein: 13 grams

94. Dehydrated Strawberries

Preparation Time: 30 minutes

Cooking Time: 6 to 12 hours

Servings: 8 to 12

Ingredients:

2 quarts fresh strawberries

2 cups water

1 cup light corn syrup

1 cup granulated sugar

Directions:

Clean the strawberries then remove the stems and slice them to ¼-inch thick.

Whisk together the water, corn syrup and sugar in a medium saucepan equipped with a stainless-steel blanching basket.

Bring the mixture to a boil then add the prepared strawberries.

Reduce the heat and simmer for 5 to 10 minutes then drain the berries.

Rinse the strawberries in cool water then spread the slices in a single layer on your dehydrator trays.

Dehydrate the strawberries for 6 to 12 hours at a temperature of 130°F (54°C) – turn the slices after a few hours to make sure they dry evenly.

When the strawberry slices are firm and chewy, cool them then store in an airtight plastic or glass container in a cool, dry location.

Nutrition:

Calories: 111

Fat: 0 gram

Carbs: 25 grams

Protein: 1 gram

95. Vegetarian Lasagna

Preparation Time: 15 minutes

Cooking Time: 45 minutes

Servings: 8

Ingredients:

1 box lasagna noodles, par boiled

12-ounce ricotta cheese

12-ounce mozzarella cheese, grated

1/2 cup Parmesan cheese, grated

1/2 lb. spinach, chopped

2 cloves garlic, minced

1 cup fresh basil, chopped

1 tablespoon fresh thyme

2 tablespoons olive oil

1 large eggplant, sliced into rounds and dehydrated

2 zucchinis, sliced into rounds and dehydrated

2 yellow squash, sliced into rounds and dehydrated

1 28 ounce can San Marzano Tomatoes, crushed

Directions:

In a large bowl, combine the cheeses and stir well. In a saucepan, combine the tomatoes, garlic, basil, and olive oil over medium heat. Simmer for 10 minutes and remove from heat. Place a small amount of tomato sauce in the bottom of a baking dish and layer the eggplant, pasta, zucchini, yellow squash, and spinach. Add a layer of the cheese mixture and sauce to each layer of vegetables. Continue layering until you run out of vegetables or that pan is full. Make sure the top layer is cheese mixture. Cover with foil and bake for 30 minutes. Remove the foil and bake an additional 15 minutes.

Nutrition:

Calories: 333

Fat: 16.7 grams

Carbs: 25.6 grams

Protein: 24.7 grams

96. Tomato Cream Sauce

Preparation Time: 15 minutes

Cooking Time: 8 hours

Servings: 6

Ingredients:

1 cup tomatoes, dehydrated

1 cup heavy cream

1/4 cup yellow onion, finely chopped

2 cloves garlic, minced

1/2 cup chicken broth

2 tablespoon vegetable oil

1/2 teaspoon black pepper

Directions:

In a medium saucepan heat oil over medium heat. Add the onion and cook until translucent. Add the garlic and cook and additional two minutes. Add the tomatoes and cook several minutes. Add the chicken broth and pepper and simmer until tomatoes have broken down. Add the cream and simmer an additional five minutes before removing from heat.

Place Clean-A-Screens on the racks of your SnackMaster and spread a thin layer of the sauce onto each screen. Set your dehydrator to 135F and dehydrate for 8 hours.

Remove dried sauce from the racks and store in zip-lock bags until ready to use.

To rehydrate sauce, mix with 1/4 cup warm water and stir.

Nutrition:

Calories: 122

Fat: 12.1 grams

Carbs: 2.7 grams

Protein: 1.2 grams

97. Apple Cake

Preparation Time: 35 minutes

Cooking Time: 12 hours

Servings: 6

Ingredients:

2 1/2 cups flour

2 teaspoons baking powder

1 teaspoon baking soda

1/2 teaspoon salt

1 1/2 cups sugar

1 cup applesauce

1 teaspoon vanilla

1 cup egg whites

1 cup milk

Directions:

In a large bowl, combine the flour, baking powder, baking soda, and salt.

In another bowl, combine the sugar, applesauce, vanilla, milk and eggs. Mix until eggs are beaten.

Stir the dry mixture into the wet mixture and pour into a greased baking dish.

Set your oven to 350F and bake for 30 to 35 minutes.

Remove the cake from the oven and allow to cool. Cut cake into cubes about 2 inches wide. Place them on the racks of your Nesco SnackMaster and set to 135F. Dehydrate for 12 hours. the cake should be crunchy when finished.

To rehydrate, sprinkle boiling water onto the cake chunks and allow them to sit for 5 minutes.

Nutrition:

Calories: 440

Fat: 1.4 grams

Carbs: 97.5 grams

Protein: 11.2 grams

98. Berry Crumble

Preparation Time: 20 minutes

Cooking Time: 8 hours

Servings: 6

Ingredients:

1 cup oats

3/4 cup flour

1/2 cup brown sugar

3/4 cup white sugar

1/2 teaspoon salt

1 stick butter, cut into pieces

2 cups raspberries

2 cups blueberries

2 cups blackberries

1/2 teaspoon cinnamon

Directions:

Place the berries on the racks of your Nesco SnackMaster and set to 125F. Dehydrate for 8 hours.

In a large bowl, combine the oats, 1/2 cup of flour, 1/2 cup white sugar, brown sugar, and salt. Add the butter and stir until butter is fully incorporated. Place the mixture in a baking dish and set your oven to 350F. Bake for 1 hour and remove to cool.

When the berries are finished dehydrating, remove from the SnackMaster and place in a zip-lock bag with the remaining flour, sugar, and cinnamon.

When ready to rehydrate, add 1/4 cup boiling water to the bag with the berries and stir until rehydrated. Top with crumble topping and serve.

Nutrition:

Calories: 453

Fat: 17 grams

Carbs: 74.7 grams

Protein: 5.1 grams

99. Roast Chicken with Dried Citrus

Preparation Time: 20 minutes

Cooking Time: 2 1/2 hours

Servings: 6

Ingredients:

1 whole chicken

1 orange, sliced into rounds and dehydrated

1 lemon, sliced into rounds and dehydrated

1 sprig fresh thyme

1 sprig fresh rosemary

4 tablespoons butter

Salt and black pepper

Directions:

Rinse and dry the chicken and place in a roasting pan. Set your oven to 375F.

Place the herbs, 2 tablespoons of butter, and three slices each of lemon and orange in the cavity of the chicken.

Place the remaining butter under the skin on the breasts of the chicken. Lay the additional citrus slices on the skin of the chicken and place in the oven for 2 hours.

Use and instant read thermometer to make sure the chicken is 165F. If not, cook an additional 30 minutes.

Nutrition:

Calories: 230

Fat: 17.2 grams

Carbs: 5.7 grams

Protein: 14.6 grams

100. Chicken Bouillon Powder

Preparation Time: 2 hours

Cooking Time: 24 hours

Servings: 20

Ingredients:

1 whole chicken, cut into pieces

1 cup dehydrated Mirepoix

Directions:

Heat a large pot of water and add the chicken pieces, cooking covered for 1 1/2 hours. Remove the chicken pieces from the broth and continue cooking uncovered until the broth has reduced to about 2 cups.

Place Clean-A-Screens on the racks of your SnackMaster. Set to 150F. and dehydrate for 24 hours or until the broth has become a solid, dry wafer.

Remove dried broth from racks and combine with the dried Mirepoix in a blender. Blend until a fine powder form. Store in jars or zip-lock bags until ready to use.

To rehydrate broth, combine 1 tablespoon of broth powder with 1 cup boiling water.

Nutrition:

Calories: 55

Fat: 3.2 grams

Carbs: 0.3 grams

Protein: 5.8 grams

101. Beef and Vegetable Soup

Preparation Time: 10 minutes

Cooking Time: 12 hours

Servings: 6

Ingredients:

1 lb. beef chuck roast, cut into chunks

2 carrots, chopped

1/2 cup green beans, chopped

1 russet potato, cubed

1/2 cup peas

1/2 cup celery

1 yellow onion, chopped

1 tablespoon salt and black pepper

Directions:

Place the beef on the racks of your dehydrator and set to 165F. Dehydrate for 6 hours or until completely dried. Remove from dehydrator.

Place carrots, green beans, potatoes, peas, celery, and onion on the racks of the SnackMaster and set to 135F. Dehydrate for 6 hours or until completely dried. In a large zip-lock bag, combine the beef, vegetables, salt, and pepper. Store until ready to use.

To make soup, combine the contents of the bag with 3 cups boiling water. Simmer until beef is cooked through and vegetables are tender.

Nutrition:

Calories: 322

Fat: 21.1 grams

Carbs: 10.9 grams

Protein: 21.7 grams

102. Apple Mint Tea

Preparation Time: 15 minutes

Cooking Time: 12 hours

Servings: 12

Ingredients:

1 red delicious apple

1 bunch fresh mint

1 cup black or green tea

Directions:

Slice apples into thin 1/8-inch slices. Wash the mint and remove the leaves from the stems.

Place the apple slices and mint leaves on the racks of your Nesco SnackMaster. Set your SnackMaster to 135F. and dehydrate for 12 hours. When the apple slices are completely dry, remove from the SnackMaster and chop the apples into small pieces.

In a medium bowl, combine the apple, mint, and tea leaves. Mix well and store in jars or zip-lock bags.

To brew a cup of tea, boil 8 ounces of water and use one teaspoon of tea blend per cup. Pour the boiling water over the tea or use an infuser. Steep for five minutes and enjoy.

Nutrition:

Calories: 5

Fat: 0.1 gram

Carbs: 3 grams

Protein: 0.2 grams

103. Maple Granola

Preparation Time: 24 hours

Cooking Time: 24 hours

Servings: 8

Ingredients:

1 cup coconut

2 cups raw almonds

2 cups walnuts

1 cup pecans

1 cup cashews

1 1/2 cup maple syrup

1/4 cup melted coconut oil

2 tablespoons vanilla

2 tablespoons cinnamon

2 tablespoons salt

Directions:

1. In a large bowl, combine nuts and cover with water. Add salt, stir and allow to sit for 24 hours.

2. Drain the nuts and dry the nuts with paper towels. Place the nuts in a food processor and pulse until the nuts are broken down into small pieces.

3. Transfer nut mixture to a large bowl and stir in the maple syrup, coconut oil, cinnamon, and vanilla. Stir well.

4. Place Clean-A-Screens on the racks of your SnackMaster and evenly spread the nut mixture. Set your SnackMaster to 125F and dehydrate for 24 hours.

5. Remove granola from the screens and allow to cool before storing.

Nutrition:

Calories: 792

Fat: 58.6 grams

Carbs: 59 grams

Protein: 17.3 grams

104. Fruit and Nut Couscous

Preparation Time: 15 minutes

Cooking Time: 3 to 5 hours

Servings: 4

Ingredients:

¾ cup water

¾ cup coconut milk

1 tablespoon agave

½ teaspoon salt

1 cup couscous

¾ cup dried peaches, diced

½ cup dried blueberries

½ cup finely chopped skinned hazelnuts

Directions:

In a medium pot, combine the water, coconut milk, agave, and salt. Bring the mixture to a boil. Add the couscous, peaches, and blueberries to the pot, then remove the pot from the heat and stir the mixture. Cover the pot and set it aside for 5 minutes. Fluff the couscous with a fork and stir in the hazelnuts. Spread the couscous mixture out evenly on the dehydrator trays fitted with a solid plastic tray insert. Place the trays in the dehydrator. Set the dehydrator to 135°F and turn it on. If your dehydrator has a built-in timer, set it for 3 hours. For models without a timer, set a separate timer. At the 3-hour mark, check the couscous. It should be firm and not feel moist. If necessary, continue to dry the couscous for another 1 to 2 hours.

Nutrition:

Calories: 450

Fat: 18 grams

Carbs: 66 grams

Protein: 10 grams

105. Dehydrated Peaches & Honey

Preparation Time: 20 minutes

Cooking Time: 25 hours

Servings: 40

Ingredients:

1 cup of honey

3 quarts peeled and pitted peaches

1 teaspoon cayenne

1 teaspoon salt

Directions:

Put the peaches in a food processor and slightly pulse them into a juicy mess. Transfer the mashed peaches to a saucepan and place it over medium heat.

Add the honey, cayenne and salt to the pan, stir everything and bring to a boil. As the peach pieces become tender, keep squashing them using the back of a spoon.

Remove from heat and allow the mixture to cool. When cooled, transfer it to the food processor again and puree into a sauce.

Transfer back the pureed mixture to the saucepan and let it cook on medium-high heat until it thickens and reduces to half.

Remove the sauce from the heat and allow it to cool slightly. Meanwhile, line your dehydrator tray with parchment paper. Evenly spread the sauce over the tray and dry at 135 degrees for 18 – 24 hours.

When ready, remove the leather from the dehydrator and peel off the parchment paper. Then cut the leather into 6-inch-wide strips. Now you can either roll them or enjoy as strips.

Nutrition:

Calories: 68

Fat: 0 gram

Carbs: 0 gram

Protein: 0 gram

106. Dehydrated Fruit Chews

Preparation Time: 15 minutes

Cooking Time: 12 hours

Servings: 12

Ingredients:

1 cup cranberries cut into pieces

2 cups rhubarb cut into pieces

1 tablespoon lemon juice

2 – 4 tablespoons honey

2 – 4 tablespoons of water

Directions:

Place a deep medium sized saucepan over low heat and pour the water in it.

Now add the cut fruits, lemon juice and honey to the pan and cover it. Let the ingredients cook over low heat until the sauce thickens.

Remove from heat and allow the mixture to get cooled. After it cools to room temperature, pour the mixture in a food processor and puree it.

Prepare your dehydrator as per manufacturer's instructions and line it with parchment paper.

Spread the cooked fruit mixture evenly on the parchment paper in the dehydrator and dry at 135 degrees for 6 – 11 hours. Turn the fruit leather when required to ensure even drying.

Peel the fruit leather off the parchment paper and cut into strips. Store or enjoy instantly.

Nutrition:

Calories: 79

Fat: 1 gram

Carbs: 18 grams

Protein: 0 gram

107 Dehydrated Veggie Falafel

Preparation Time: 30 minutes

Cooking Time: 12 hours

Servings: 2 to 3

Ingredients:

1 cup dry sunflower seeds

2 cups roughly chopped carrots

1/3 cup flax seeds, ground

1/2 cup sesame seeds

3 tablespoons diced onion

1 clove minced garlic

1 cup fresh parsley, well chopped

1/2 teaspoon cumin

1/2 teaspoon curry

1/4 teaspoon salt

Directions:

Put the sunflower seeds, flax seeds, cumin, curry, salt and garlic in a grinder or food processor and pulse until well ground.

Now add the chopped carrots and pulse again till the mixture resembles a coarse paste.

Next add the parsley and onion and again grind while scraping the mixer as needed.

Transfer the mixture to a large bowl and add the sesame seeds. Mix everything using your hands and then start rolling the mixture into small bite-sized balls.

Prepare the dehydrator as per manufacturer's instructions and place the falafel balls on the sheets. Dehydrate for up to 12 hours. Store or enjoy instantly.

Nutrition:

Calories: 130

Fat: 6 grams

Carbs: 18 grams

Protein: 1 gram

108. Dehydrated Potato Hash browns

Preparation Time: 30 minutes

Cooking Time: 4 to 5 hours

Servings: 6

Ingredients:

10 potatoes

1 cup lemon juice

Directions:

Wash the potatoes and peel off the outer skin. Place the peeled potatoes in cool water for some time. Now grate the potatoes using a grater. Place a deep pot 3/4th filled with water on medium heat and put the grated potatoes in a colander. Place the colander over the pot with the heating water such that the potatoes immerse in the water. Boil the potatoes in this way for 3 – 4 minutes. Lower the flame, remove the colander from the pot and run cold water through the boiled potatoes to drain away the starch. Then replace the colander over the pot on the gas. Pour cold water over the potatoes in the colander placed on top of the pot to cover them and also pour in the lemon juice. Toss the potatoes gently in the water and lemon juice mixture and let them cook in this mixture for about 45 minutes. Remove the colander from the heat and drain off the water. Now dry the potatoes by emptying the colander on a clean towel and squeezing out as much water from the potatoes as possible. Now spread the grated boiled potatoes on dehydrator sheets and dry until they become crispy. For preparing hash browns, put about 2 cups of the dried grated potatoes in a bowl and cover them with warm water for 15 – 20 minutes. Then fry them. Serve.

Nutrition:

Calories: 180

Fat: 11 grams

Carbs: 15 grams

Protein: 2 grams

109. Dehydrated Coconut & Lemon Macaroons

Preparation Time: 30 minutes

Cooking Time: 6 to 8 hours

Servings: 18

Ingredients:

1 1/2 cup dried, shredded unsweetened coconut

1/4 cup coconut oil, gently melted

30-40 drops organic, food-grade lemon essential oil

3/4 cup almond flour

1/4 cup plus 1-2 tablespoons raw honey

Pinch of unrefined sea salt

Directions:

In a large bowl combine all the ingredients nicely. The final consistency should be loose dough like.

Scoop out small portions of the dough using a deep round spoon or small ice-cream spoon and invert the rounded dough on parchment paper. It will look like a semi-circle placed flat side down.

Place the parchment paper in the dehydrator and dry the macaroons until they become slightly dry on the outside and chewy on the inside.

Remove from the dehydrator when done and cool them slightly before serving.

Nutrition:

Calories: 89

Fat: 0 grams

Carbs: 0 grams

Protein: 0 grams

110. Beef Bell Pepper Soup

Preparation Time: 15 minutes

Cooking Time: 30 minutes

Servings: 6

Ingredients:

½ cup freeze-dried ground beef

¾ cup instant brown rice

¼ cup dried celery

1/3 cup dehydrated sliced onion

1 cup dehydrated bell peppers

1 tablespoon beef bouillon

1 teaspoon garlic powder

¾ cup tomato powder

¼ cup freeze dried sausage crumbled

9 cups water

Directions:

Add all ingredients except water into the glass jar. Seal jar tightly with lid.

To cook: Add water and jar content to the saucepan and bring to boil.

Reduce heat and simmer for 15-20 minutes.

Serve and enjoy.

Nutrition:

Calories: 171

Fat: 2.3 grams

Carbs: 32.3 grams

Protein: 6.9 grams

111. Chicken Tortilla Soup

Preparation Time: 10 minutes

Cooking Time: 30 minutes

Servings: 6

Ingredients:

1 cup dehydrated chicken

¼ teaspoon ground chipotle pepper

1 cup dried corn

2/3 cup dried green chilies

½ cup dehydrated sliced onion

1 teaspoon garlic powder

2 teaspoons chicken bouillon

1 ½ tablespoon chili powder

½ cup tomato powder

8 cups water

Directions:

Add all ingredients into the glass jar. Seal jar tightly with lid and shake well.

To cook: Add water and jar content to the saucepan and bring to boil.

Reduce heat and simmer for 15-20 minutes.

Serve with tortilla chips.

Nutrition:

Calories: 120

Fat: 1.6 grams

Carbs: 19.2 grams

Protein: 9.8 grams

112. Minestrone Soup

Preparation Time: 10 minutes

Cooking Time: 22 minutes

Servings: 4

Ingredients:

¼ cup dehydrated corn

¼ cup dehydrated bell peppers

¼ cup dehydrated carrots

¼ cup dehydrated peas

¼ cup dehydrated green beans

¼ cup dehydrated sliced onion

¼ cup dehydrated celery

¾ cup pasta

1 tablespoon dried beef bouillon

1 teaspoon dried parsley

½ teaspoon Italian seasoning

¼ cup tomato powder

6 cups water

Directions:

Add all ingredients except water into the glass jar. Seal jar tightly with lid and shake well.

To cook: Add water and jar content to the saucepan and bring to boil.

Reduce heat and simmer for 12 minutes or until vegetable and pasta are cooked.

Serve and enjoy.

Nutrition:

Calories: 128

Fat: 1 gram

Carbs: 28.1 grams

Protein: 3.6 grams

113. Chicken Noodle Soup

Preparation Time: 10 minutes

Cooking Time: 35 minutes

Servings: 4

Ingredients:

¼ cup red lentils

1 bay leaf

1 cup egg noodles

1/8 teaspoon celery seed

1/8 teaspoon garlic powder

½ teaspoon dill seed

1 ½ tablespoon chicken bouillon granules

2 tablespoon dehydrated sliced onion

8 cups water

Directions:

Add all ingredients except water into the glass jar. Seal jar with lid tightly and shake well.

To cook: Add water and jar content to the saucepan and bring to boil.

Reduce heat and simmer for 25 minutes.

Serve and enjoy.

Nutrition:

Calories: 108

Fat: 1.1 gram

Carbs: 19.6 grams

Protein: 5.2 grams

114. Perfect Lamb Jerky

Preparation Time: 10 minutes

Cooking Time: 6 hours

Servings: 6

Ingredients:

2 ½ lbs. boneless lamb, trimmed fat and slice into thin strips

½ teaspoon black pepper

1 tablespoon oregano

1 teaspoon garlic powder

1 ½ teaspoon onion powder

3 tablespoons Worcestershire sauce

1/3 cup soy sauce

Directions:

Add soy sauce, Worcestershire sauce, onion powder, garlic powder, oregano, and black pepper in the large bowl and mix well.

Add meat slices in the bowl and mix until well coated. Cover bowl tightly and place in refrigerator for overnight.

Arrange marinated meat slices on dehydrator racks and dehydrate to 145 F/ 63 C for 5-6 hours.

Nutrition:

Calories: 373

Fat: 14 grams

Carbs: 4 grams

Protein: 54.2 grams

115. Venison Jerky

Preparation Time: 30 minutes

Cooking Time: 4 to 8 hours

Servings: 6

Ingredients:

2 lbs. Venison Steak, fat removed

¼ cup Worcestershire Sauce

¼ cup Soy Sauce

1½ teaspoon Liquid Smoke

1 teaspoon Onion Powder

½ teaspoon Garlic Powder

½ teaspoon Crushed Garlic

½ teaspoon Smoked Pepper

¼ teaspoon Chili Powder

1 tablespoon Ground Coriander

½ teaspoon Cracked Pepper

1 teaspoon Sea Salt

Directions:

Slice the meat into thin slices and place in a sealable bag.

Whisk together the remaining ingredients and pour into the bag with the meat. Toss to coat the meat and keep in the fridge for 24-48 hours to marinate. Toss a few times during this time.

Pat dry the meat and arrange on dehydrator trays. Dehydrate at 150F / 65C for 4-8 hours depending on the thickness of the strips.

Allow to cool and store in airtight containers.

Nutrition:

Calories: 265.6

Fat: 4.0 grams

Carbs: 2.9 grams

Protein: 51.0 grams

116. Chinese Pork Jerky

Preparation Time: 30 minutes

Cooking Time: 6 to 10 hours

Servings: 6

Ingredients:

2 lbs. Ground Pork

2 tablespoon Shao Hsing Cooking Wine

1 tablespoon Dark Soy Sauce

1 tablespoon Fish Sauce

1 teaspoon Sesame Oil

½ teaspoon Ground Pepper

½ teaspoon Five-Spice Powder

2/3 cups Sugar

Directions:

Add the ingredients to a large bowl and mix to combine. Cover and keep in the fridge for at least 4 hours.

Line dehydrator trays with parchment paper and spread the mixture into thin layers. Cover with parchment paper and gently press to even out and smoothen the meat strips.

Dehydrate at 145F / 62C for 6 hours. Flip and dehydrate for a few more hours until dried.

Allow to cool and store in airtight containers

Nutrition:

Calories: 533.1

Fat: 34.6 grams

Carbs: 10.0 grams

Protein: 42.8 grams

117. Raw Zucchini Bread

Preparation Time: 20 minutes

Cooking Time: 6 hours

Servings: 6

Ingredients:

2 cups Walnuts

2 teaspoons Cinnamon

1 1/2 cup Dates

1 teaspoon Vanilla Extract

3 cups Grated Zucchini

1 cup Shredded Unsweetened Coconut

1/2 cup Raisins

1/2 cup Psyllium Husk

Directions:

Add the walnuts to your food processor and pulse until ground. Add the cinnamon, dates, and vanilla and process until combined. Transfer to a bowl, add the zucchini, coconut, raisins, and psyllium husk and mix well to combine. Use the mixture to make 10 loaves and place them on the dehydrator trays lined with parchment paper. Dehydrate at 150F/65C for an hour, reduce the temperature to 110F/43C and dehydrate for 5 more hours. When done, allow to cool and store in the fridge.

Nutrition:

Calories: 373.7

Fat: 22.5 grams

Carbs: 45.9 grams

Protein: 6.9 grams

118. Black Bread

Preparation Time: 30 minutes

Cooking Time: 8 to 12 hours

Servings: 4

Ingredients:

2 Garlic Cloves, peeled

1/4 cup Water

1 teaspoon Lemon Juice

1/4 cup Chopped Red Onion

1 tablespoon Agave Nectar

1 tablespoon Cacao Powder

1/4 cup Ground Flax Seeds

1 tablespoon Caraway seeds

1/4 teaspoon Black Pepper

1 cup Raw Walnuts, soaked overnight, rinsed and drained

1 cup Buckwheat Groats, soaked overnight, rinsed and drained

Directions:

Add the walnuts and buckwheat groats to your blender or food processor and pulse until chopped. Add the garlic, water, lemon juice, onion, and agave nectar and pulse until combined.

Transfer to a bowl and mix in the cacao, flaxseed meal, caraway seeds, and pepper.

Pour the dough onto a dehydrator sheet, spread it until it is ¼-inch thick and score it into squares or rectangles.

Dehydrate at 115F / 46C for 8 to 12 depending on the preferred doneness.

When done, break into pieces and store in airtight containers.

Nutrition:

Calories: 324.1

Fat: 18.7 grams

Carbs: 38.4 grams

Protein: 9.8 grams

119. Cauliflower Popcorn

Preparation Time: 30 minutes

Cooking Time: 12 to 24 hours

Servings: 4

Ingredients:

½ cup Water

3 tablespoons Nutritional Yeast

1 cup Dates

2 tablespoons Tahini

2 teaspoons Garlic Powder

1 tablespoon Apple Cider Vinegar

1-2 teaspoons Cayenne Pepper

2 teaspoons Onion Powder

½ teaspoon Turmeric

2 heads of Cauliflower, separated into florets and chopped

¼ cup Sun-Dried Tomatoes, soaked in warm water for an hour

Directions:

Add the ingredients to your blender and blend until smooth and thick. Transfer to a large bowl and set aside.

Add the chopped cauliflower and toss to coat.

Arrange the cauliflower on dehydrator trays and dehydrate at 115F / 46C for about 12 or up to 24 hours until the desired doneness.

Allow to cool and store in airtight containers.

Nutrition:

Calories: 197.4

Fat: 0.9 grams

Carbs: 17.3 grams

Protein: 6.9 grams

120. Paleo Granola

Preparation Time: 20 minutes

Cooking Time: 6 to 8 hours

Servings: 6

Ingredients:

2 cups Hazelnuts, chopped

1/2 cup Cashews

1/2 cup Pumpkin Seeds, chopped

2 tablespoons Sesame Seeds

2 tablespoons Coconut Oil, melted

1/4 cup Honey

2 tablespoons Almond Butter

1 teaspoon Vanilla Extract

1 teaspoon Cinnamon

1/4 teaspoon Ginger Powder

1/2 teaspoon Celtic Sea Salt

3/4 cup Unsweetened Coconut Flakes

1/4 cup Raw Cacao Nibs

1/2 cup Dried Cranberries or Raisins

Directions:

Mix together the honey, coconut oil, and butter into a paste. Stir in the cinnamon, vanilla, ginger, and salt.

Add the nuts and seeds and stir well to coat the nuts. Sprinkle with the coconut and mix well.

Spread on your dehydrator trays and dehydrate at 115F / 46C for 6-8 hours or until dry and crunchy.

Add the dried fruits and cacao nibs and store in airtight containers.

Nutrition:

Calories: 579.3

Fat: 42.1 grams

Carbs: 50.0 grams

Protein: 11.6 grams

Chapter 8: Chapter 12: Advanced Recipes

121. Crispy Tofu with Roasted Sweet Potatoes and Rice

Preparation Time: 10 minutes

Cooking Time: 30 minutes

Serving: 4

Ingredients:

1 cup brown rice, rinsed

¾ cup water

1 sweet potato, peeled and diced

2 tablespoons extra-virgin olive oil, divided

1 teaspoon sea salt

1 teaspoon freshly ground black pepper

1 (15-ounce) block organic extra-firm tofu, drained and sliced into ½-inch cubes

1 tablespoon soy sauce

2 teaspoons cornstarch

Directions:

Place the rice and water in the pot and stir to combine. Assemble the Pressure Lid, making sure the pressure release valve is in the Seal position. Select Pressure and set to High. Set the time to 2 minutes, then select Start/Stop to begin.

While the rice is cooking, in a small mixing bowl, toss the sweet potato in 1 tablespoon of olive oil and season with the salt and black pepper.

Ensure that the tofu is well-drained, and all excess water is removed. In a medium mixing bowl, whisk together the remaining 1 tablespoon of olive oil and the soy sauce. Toss the tofu cubes in the soy sauce mixture, then add the cornstarch and toss until evenly coated.

When pressure cooking the rice is complete, quick release the pressure by moving the pressure release valve to the Vent position. Carefully remove the lid when the pressure has finished releasing.

Place the Reversible Rack in the pot in the higher position and line with aluminum foil. Arrange the sweet potatoes and tofu on the rack.

Close the Crisping Lid. Select Air Crisp, set the temperature to 400°F, and set the time to 20 minutes. Select Start/Stop to begin. Use tongs to flip the sweet potatoes and tofu after 10 minutes.

When cooking is complete, check for your desired crispiness and serve.

Nutrition:

Calories: 328

Fat: 10 grams

Carbs: 47 grams

Protein: 12g

122. Lemon Risotto and Roasted Carrots

Preparation Time: 10 minutes

Cooking Time: 34 minutes

Serving: 4

Ingredients:

2 tablespoons extra-virgin olive oil, divided

1 garlic clove, minced

5 cups vegetable broth

¼ cup freshly squeezed lemon juice

1 teaspoon grated lemon zest

2 cups Arborio rice

2 teaspoons sea salt, divided

4 carrots, cut ¾ inch thick on the diagonal

1 teaspoon freshly ground black pepper

2 tablespoons unsalted butter

1½ cups grated Parmesan cheese, plus more for garnish

Directions:

Select Sear/Sauté and set to Medium High. Select Start/Stop to begin. Allow the pot to preheat for 5 minutes.

Add 1 tablespoon of oil and the garlic to the preheated pot and cook until fragrant, about 1 minute. Add the broth, lemon juice, lemon zest, and rice to the pot. Season with 1 teaspoon of salt and stir to combine.

Assemble the Pressure Lid, making sure the pressure release valve is in the Seal position. Select Pressure and set to High. Set the time to 7 minutes, then select Start/Stop to begin.

While the rice is cooking, in a medium mixing bowl, toss together the carrots with the remaining 1 tablespoon of oil, the remaining 1 teaspoon of salt, and the black pepper.

When pressure cooking is complete, allow the pressure to naturally release for 10 minutes, then quick release any remaining pressure by moving the pressure release valve to the Vent position. Carefully remove the lid when the unit has finished releasing pressure.

Stir the butter into the rice until evenly incorporated. Place the Reversible Rack inside the pot over the risotto, making sure the rack is in the higher position. Place the carrots on the rack.

Close the Crisping Lid. Select Broil and set the time to 8 minutes. Select Start/Stop to begin.

When cooking is complete, remove the rack from the pot. Stir the Parmesan cheese into the risotto. Top with the roasted carrots and garnish with additional Parmesan. Serve immediately.

Nutrition:

Calories: 674

Fat: 24 grams

Carbs: 92 grams

Protein: 22 grams

123. Chickpea, Spinach, and Sweet Potato Stew

Preparation Time: 15 minutes

Cooking Time: 23 minutes

Serving: 6

Ingredients:

1 tablespoon extra-virgin olive oil

1 yellow onion, diced

4 garlic cloves, minced

4 sweet potatoes, peeled and diced

4 cups vegetable broth

1 (15-ounce) can fire-roasted diced tomatoes, undrained

2 (15-ounce) cans chickpeas, drained

1½ teaspoons ground cumin

1 teaspoon ground coriander

½ teaspoon paprika

½ teaspoon sea salt

½ teaspoon freshly ground black pepper

4 cups baby spinach

Directions:

Select Sear/Sauté and set to Medium High. Select Start/Stop to begin. Allow the pot to preheat for 5 minutes.

Combine the oil, onion, and garlic in the pot. Cook, stirring occasionally, for 5 minutes.

Black pepper to the pot. Assemble the Pressure Lid, making sure the pressure release valve is in the Seal position.

Select Pressure and set to High. Set the time to 8 minutes, then select Start/Stop to begin.

When pressure cooking is complete, quick release the pressure by moving the pressure release valve to the Vent position. Carefully remove the lid when the unit has finished releasing pressure.

Add the spinach to the pot and stir until wilted. Serve.

Nutrition:

Calories: 220

Fat: 4 grams

Carbs: 42 grams

Protein: 7 grams

124. Dehydrated Almond Cherry Granola Bars

Preparation Time: 30 minutes

Cooking Time: 16 hours

Servings: 12

Ingredients:

1 cup whole oat groats

1 cup raw almonds

1 cup raw pumpkin seeds, hulled

1 cup dried cherries

1 cup whole flaxseed

2 tablespoons coconut oil

½ cup raw honey

½ cup ground flaxseed

¼ cup raw sesame seeds

1 cup pitted Medjool dates, chopped

Directions:

Place your groats, almonds and pumpkin seeds in separate bowls.

Pour in enough water to cover the ingredients then soak overnight.

Drain the bowls then place the groats in a food processor and blend into a damp powder.

Add the sunflower seeds and almonds then pulse until ground.

Transfer the ingredients to a mixing bowl and stir in the cherries and whole flaxseed.

In a separate bowl, whisk together the coconut oil, honey, ground flaxseed and sesame seeds.

Transfer the mixture to a food processor and add the dates.

Blend until thick and well combined then pour into the mixing bowl with the other ingredients and stir well.

Spread the mixture on a lined dehydrator tray as evenly as possible.

Use a knife to score the mixture in 3-by-3-inch squares.

Dehydrate for 2 hours at 145°F (63°C) then reduce temperature to 125°F and dry for 8 hours or overnight – turn the bars once halfway through.

When completely dried, cut the mixture into bars and store in airtight containers.

Nutrition:

Calories: 160

Fat: 5 grams

Carbs: 24 grams

Protein: 7 grams

125. Dried Cranberry Oat Bars

Preparation Time: 30 minutes

Cooking Time:

Servings:

Ingredients:

1 cup whole oat groats

1 cup raw sunflower seeds

1 cup raw walnut halves

1 cup dried cranberries

½ cup whole flaxseed

½ cup raw sesame seeds

2 tablespoons coconut oil

1/3 cup raw honey

¾ cups ground flaxseed

1 cup pitted Medjool dates, chopped

Directions:

Place your groats, sunflower seeds and walnuts in separate bowls.

Pour in enough water to cover the ingredients then soak overnight.

Drain the bowls then place the groats in a food processor and blend into a damp powder.

Add the sunflower seeds and walnuts then pulse until ground.

Transfer the ingredients to a mixing bowl and stir in the cranberries, whole flaxseed and sesame seeds.

In a separate bowl, whisk together the coconut oil, honey and ground flaxseed.

Transfer the mixture to a food processor and add the dates.

Blend until thick and well combined then pour into the mixing bowl with the other ingredients and stir well.

Spread the mixture on a lined dehydrator tray as evenly as possible.

Use a knife to score the mixture in 3-by-3-inch squares.

Dehydrate for 2 hours at 145°F (63°C) then reduce temperature to 125°F (52°C) and dry for 8 hours or overnight – turn the bars once halfway through.

When completely dried, cut the mixture into bars and store in airtight containers.

Nutrition:

Calories: 120

Fat: 4 grams

Carbs: 19 grams

Protein: 3 grams

126. Ground Turkey Jerky

Preparation Time: 20 minutes

Cooking Time: 4 to 6 hours

Servings: 6

Ingredients:

Zest and juice of 1 lemon

1 tablespoon agave

1 tablespoon Worcestershire sauce

2 teaspoons apple cider vinegar

1 garlic clove, minced

1 teaspoon salt

1 teaspoon freshly ground black pepper

½ teaspoon dried thyme

1-pound ground turkey, at least 93 percent lean

Directions:

In a medium bowl, combine the lemon zest and juice, agave, Worcestershire sauce, vinegar, garlic, salt, pepper, and thyme and stir well to mix. Add the turkey to the bowl and knead the mixture with your hands until all the ingredients are thoroughly combined. Cover the bowl and chill the mixture in the refrigerator for 30 minutes to 2 hours.

Remove the bowl from the refrigerator, turn out the turkey mixture onto a sheet of waxed or parchment paper, and flatten the mixture slightly. Cover with an additional piece of wax or parchment paper and flatten the turkey mixture with a rolling pin or your hands until the mixture is ½ inch thick.

Remove the top piece of paper and cut the turkey mixture into strips 1 inch wide and about 5 inches long.

Arrange the strips of turkey mix onto mesh dehydrator trays, leaving a little space between each strip. (Wetting your knife or spatula and hands occasionally keeps the turkey from sticking as you transfer the strips.) Make sure that the strips are not stretched out too thinly, and fill in any holes so the strips maintain a ½-inch thickness.

Place the trays in the dehydrator. Set the dehydrator to 150°F and turn it on. If your dehydrator has a built-in timer, set it for 4 hours. For models without a timer, set a separate timer.

At the 4-hour mark, check the turkey strips. The jerky is ready when it can bend but not break apart and does not feel moist. If necessary, continue to dry the strips for another 1 to 2 hours.

Preheat the oven to 250°F. Place the strips on a baking sheet and bake for 10 minutes to ensure the meat is free of bacteria.

Nutrition:

Calories: 60

Fat: 1 gram

Carbs: 0 gram

Protein: 11 grams

127. Salmon Jerky

Preparation Time: 25 minutes

Cooking Time: 4 to 6 hours

Servings: 6

Ingredients:

1 (1½-pound) salmon fillet

½ cup soy sauce or tamari

2 tablespoons brown sugar

½ teaspoon freshly ground black pepper

½ teaspoon smoked paprika

1 garlic clove, minced

1 tablespoon freshly squeezed lemon juice

Directions:

Freeze the salmon fillet for 30 minutes before cutting, for easier slicing.

Mix the soy sauce, sugar, pepper, paprika, garlic, and lemon juice in a small bowl.

Remove any pin bones from the salmon and slice it into ¼-inch strips.

Combine the salmon strips and marinade in a gallon-size zip-sealed bag and gently knead to mix the salmon with the marinade. Chill the bag in the refrigerator for 4 hours.

Preheat the oven to 250°F. Remove the salmon from the bag and discard the marinade. Place the salmon strips on a baking sheet and bake for 10 minutes. This brings the internal temperature of the salmon to 160°F for safety. A digital thermometer is handy for checking the internal temperature of the salmon.

Place the salmon strips on mesh dehydrator trays, leaving a little space between each strip.

Place the trays in the dehydrator. Set the dehydrator to 160°F and turn it on. If your dehydrator has a built-in timer, set it for 4 hours. For models without a timer, set a separate timer.

Periodically check the salmon, and if necessary, use a paper towel to absorb any oil from the surface of the salmon.

At the 4-hour mark, check the salmon. Salmon will dehydrate more quickly than red meat. The salmon is ready when it can bend but not break, and it should be slightly chewy, not crispy. If necessary, continue to dry the salmon for another 1 to 2 hours, checking often for doneness.

Nutrition:

Calories: 90

Fat: 2 grams

Carbs: 6 grams

Protein: 13 grams

128. Dehydrated Risotto

Preparation Time: 30 minutes

Cooking Time: 9 hours

Servings: 2 to 3

Ingredients:

1 cup Short Grain Rice

2 cups Chicken or Vegetable Broth

1/2 cup White Wine

1 cup Mushrooms, sliced or diced

1/2medium Red Onion, chopped

1 clove Garlic, minced

3 tablespoons Parmesan Cheese

1 tablespoon Olive Oil

1 pinch Saffron

Directions:

Place a deep pot over medium heat and add some olive oil to it. Once the oil is heated, add the onions and garlic to it and cook until they become translucent.

Meanwhile, boil the broth in a separate pot over medium heat.

Add the rice to the pot with the onions and garlic and stir continuously for 1 minute.

Pour the white wine into this pot and stir continuously until it is absorbed.

Now add the mushrooms and the boiled broth, 1/2 cup at a time to the pot. Allow the liquid in the pot to be absorbed before adding more. Stir gently continuously.

Now remove the pot from the heat and allow the risotto to cool down. Once it has cooled, spread it out on dehydrator sheets.

Dry for about 3 hours and then separate any rice grains sticking to each other. Dry for another 4 hours. Then rub the risotto grains within your palms to separate them even more. Dry for another 1 hour.

When the risotto is dried, transfer small quantities of it to packing container. Pack the parmesan cheese in small plastic bags and place along with the risotto in the packing containers.

Nutrition:

Calories: 50

Fat:

Carbs: 11 grams

Protein: 1 gram

129. Dehydrated Vegetable Broth

Preparation Time: 1 hour

Cooking Time: 21 hours

Servings: 3 to 4

Ingredients:

16 – 32ounces Chicken Broth

1-pound Parsnips

1 large Sweet Potato

3 medium Turnips

1 large Rutabaga

14.5-ounce Tomatoes, drained and diced

2 medium Onions, chopped

2 cloves Garlic, minced

1/4 cup Raisins

1 tablespoon Curry Powder

1 tablespoon Ground Cumin

1 teaspoon Cinnamon

1 tablespoon Olive Oil

Salt and pepper for taste

Directions:

Clean the parsnips, sweet potato, turnips and rutabaga and dice them into 1/2-inch cubes.

Place a non-stick saucepan over medium heat and add olive oil to it. When the oil is hot enough, add the onions to it and sauté for 5 minutes or until the onions turn golden brown.

Now add the cinnamon, cumin, curry powder, garlic and a little broth to the pan and stir. Let the mixture cook for 1 – 2 minutes.

Place a large pot over medium heat and pour the contents of the pan into it.

Also add the diced vegetables and raisins.

Now pour in more broth enough to cover the vegetables and raisins. Stir everything and bring the broth to a boil.

Reduce the heat, cover the pot and simmer for 10 minutes or until the vegetables become tender.

Now add the diced tomatoes and season with salt and pepper. Simmer the mixture for 5 more minutes while stirring occasionally.

Remove the pot from the heat. Place a large colander over another pot and drain the broth through the colander.

Transfer about 4 cups of the vegetables (except the raisins) with some of the drained broth to a food processor and pulse until they become smooth.

Cover your dehydrator sheet with parchment paper and spread out a thick layer of the pureed mixture on it. Dry at 135 degrees for 8 hours.

Spread out the remaining cooked veggies to dehydrator sheet covered with parchment paper and dry at 135 degrees for 12 hours. Separate any vegetables that stick together.

Allow everything to cool and then pack some of the dried broth and some of the dried veggies in small containers. Combine both with warm water when ready to serve.

Nutrition:

Calories: 10

Fat: 0 gram

Carbs: 3 grams

Protein: 0 gram

130. Pumpkin Spice Cookies

Preparation Time: 1 hour

Cooking Time: 4 to 6 hours

Servings: 6

Ingredients:

2 cups Almond Flour

2 cups Coconut Flour

2 cups Chopped Raw Pumpkin

1 cup Dates, pitted and soaked in warm water

1 3/4 cup Ground Flax Seeds

1 teaspoon Coconut Nectar

2 teaspoon Minced Ginger

1 teaspoon Vanilla Paste

1/4 teaspoon Nutmeg

2 tablespoon Cinnamon

1/4 teaspoon Cloves

1/4 teaspoon Sea Salt

1 cup Desiccated Coconut

1 cup Cashews

1/2 cup Coconut Oil

Vanilla Paste, to taste

Salt, to taste

Directions:

Combine the almond and coconut flour in a large bowl and set aside.

Add the remaining ingredients to your blender or food processor and blend until combined and smooth.

Transfer to the bowl with the flours and mix well until dough is formed.

Use the mixture to form cookies and arrange them on the dehydrator trays.

Dehydrate for 4 hours at 155F / 68C. Reduce the temperature to 108F / 42C and dehydrate the cookies until the desired doneness.

When done, allow the cookies to cool.

Add the ingredients to your blender or the food processor and pulse until smooth. Pour over the cookies and place in the fridge until the icing sets.

Nutrition:

Calories: 442.9

Fat: 24.1 grams

Carbs: 42.1 grams

Protein: 20.7 grams

131. Granola Bar Crackers

Preparation Time:

Cooking Time:

Servings: 4

Ingredients:

1 cup Ground Flax Seeds

A pinch of Cardamom

1/2 teaspoon Cinnamon

1/4 cup Unsweetened Cacao Nibs

1/2 teaspoon Orange Zest

A pinch of Salt

1-inch Fresh Ginger Root, peeled and chopped

1 cup Raw Walnuts, soaked overnight, rinsed and drained

1 large Apple, cored and chopped

1/4 cup Unsweetened Coconut Flakes, soaked in warm water for an hour and drained

1 cup Water

1/4 cup Coconut Oil

1/4 cup Agave Nectar

Directions:

Combine the flaxseed meal, cardamom, cinnamon, orange zest, cacao nibs, and salt and set aside.

Add the ginger, walnuts, and apple to your food processor or blender and pulse until pureed. Transfer to the bowl with the flaxseed mixture along with the remaining ingredients. Mix well to combine the ingredients.

Line a dehydrator tray with a non-stick sheet and pour the dough over it. Cover with another non-stick sheet, gently roll out until it is ¼-inch thick, and score it into squares or rectangles.

Remove the top non-stick sheet and dehydrate for half an hour at 145F / 62C.

Reduce the temperature to 115F / 46C and dry for 24 hours.

When done, allow to cool, break into pieces and store in airtight containers.

Nutrition:

Calories: 508.2

Fat: 42.3 grams

Carbs: 31.6 grams

Protein: 9.3 grams

132. Spicy Salsa Crackers

Preparation Time: 30 minutes

Cooking Time: 19 hours

Servings: 8

Ingredients:

1 cup Dried Quinoa, soaked in 3 cups water for 48 hours, drained

1 tablespoon Sesame Oil

1/4 cup Water

8 Garlic Cloves

1 Jalapeno

1/2 cup Corn Kernels

1 Lime, zest and juice

2 cup Pearl Tomatoes

1/2 Yellow Onion

1/4 cup Fresh Cilantro Leaves

2 tablespoon Chia Seeds, finely ground

1/2 cup Sunflower Seeds

1 teaspoon Himalayan salt

Directions:

Add the quinoa to your food processor or blender, water, and sesame oil and pulse to combine into a paste. Transfer to a bowl and set aside.

Add the jalapeno, garlic, lime juice and zest, and corn to the food processor or blender and process until smooth. Transfer to the bowl with the quinoa mix.

Add the onion, tomatoes, and cilantro leaves to the food processor or the blender, finely chop and transfer to the bowl.

Add the sunflower and chia seeds, season with the salt and stir well to combine. Allow to sit for 15 minutes.

Spread the batter onto a solid dehydrator tray and dehydrate at 115F / 46C for 5 hours. Place in a sealable container and keep in the fridge overnight.

Take out the dough from the fridge and roll it out into a ¼-inch thick rectangle. Cut the dough into crackers, arrange them on the solid dehydrator trays. Dehydrate at 115F / 46C for 5 hours.

Transfer to the mash tray and dehydrate for 9 more hours, flipping every 3 hours.

Allow to cool and store in airtight containers.

Nutrition:

Calories: 145.0

Fat: 5.5 grams

Carbs: 20.2 grams

Protein: 4.9 grams

133. Crunchy Breakfast Granola

Preparation Time: 35 minutes

Cooking Time: 8 to 32 hours

Servings: 16

Ingredients:

Water, purified

1 cup of pitted, packed dates

1/2 teaspoon of salt, sea

2 & 1/2 cups of buckwheat groats, raw – soak for 8-12 hours, then rinse & drain, then sprout

3/4 cup of currants, raisins, cranberries, dried blueberries of cherries, organic

1/4 cup of seeds, flax – soak for 8-12 hours in a half cup of the water – don't rinse or drain

1/4 cup of pumpkin seeds, raw – soak for four to six hours, then rinse & drain

1/4 cup of sunflower seeds, raw – soak for four to six hours, then rinse & drain

1/4 cup of sesame seeds, raw – soak for four to six hours, then rinse & drain

1/2 – 1 cup of whole or sliced almonds, raw – soak for eight to 12 hours

1/2 – 1 cup of pecan or walnut pieces – soak for 8-12 hours

1 cored & wedge-cut apple, large

1 tablespoon of cinnamon, ground

Directions:

Cover buckwheat groats in large bowl with one-inch purified water. Allow them to sit for eight to 12 hours.

After the groats soak for eight for 12 hours, put groats in strainer or sieve. Rinse well. Allow them to sit in strainer in sink for eight hours more, so they can sprout. Rinse them halfway through the sprouting process. Rinse again before you add to recipe.

After groats are rinsed and strained, but before they have been left to sprout, put flax seeds and 1/2 cup water in bowl. Soak for eight to 12 hours. Seeds will mix with water, becoming a gel.

Place almonds, pecans or walnuts and salt together in separate bowl. Cover with water and soak for eight to 12 hours. Rinse, then strain. They will be done sprouting at the same time buckwheat has sprouted.

About half-way into soaking time for nuts and flax seeds, combine sesame, pumpkin and sunflower seeds in bowl. Cover with water. Allow to soak for four to six hours. Rinse, then strain. They will be done at about the same time as nuts and flax seeds are done soaking and buckwheat has completed its sprouting.

After groats, seeds and nuts are done, separate dates loosely. Soak in water for several minutes and soften if they seem too dry and hard. Drain off water. Remove pits.

Place dates and wedge-cut apples in your food processor. Add 1/2 cup water. Pure into paste with smooth texture. Add additional water if you need it.

Combine flax seed gel, dried berries or currants, raisins, groats and other nuts and seeds in large sized bowl. Add cinnamon, date paste and apple puree. Mix well, creating a batter.

Spread three cups of batter evenly, 1/4" thick or less, on dehydrator tray that is lined using wax paper or a sheet of silicone. Repeat till you have used all the batter.

Dehydrate the batter at 105 to 115F for eight hours. Flip the granola on clean hydrator tray. Remove silicone sheet or wax paper. Dehydrate at 105F for 24 more hours, till dry fully.

Break granola in chunks. Store in sealed jar in refrigerator for three months maximum. You can also keep the granola in sealed jars or storage bags in your pantry for a maximum for one month. Store till ready to use.

Nutrition:

Calories: 110

Fat: 5 grams

Carbs: 15 grams

Protein: 3 grams

134. Bulgur Dehydrated Chili

Preparation Time: 40 minutes

Cooking Time: 8 to 10 hours

Servings: 1

Ingredients:

1/2 chopped onion, red

1 teaspoon of oil, olive

1/2 chopped bell pepper, red

1/2 cup of diced tomatoes, canned

1/4 cup of bulgur, quick-cooking

1 teaspoon of seasoning blend, Mexican

Salt, sea and Pepper, ground

1/4 cup of canned, drained kidney beans

1/3 ounce of chocolate, dark

Directions:

Heat oil in pan on med. heat. Add the onions. Cook till soft. Add and stir in bulgur, peppers and the Mexican seasoning blend. Cook for one to two minutes, releasing aroma. Pour in one-half cup of water and the diced tomatoes. Bring to boil and stir occasionally. Season as desired. Add kidney beans. Simmer for six to seven minutes, till nearly all the water has been absorbed. Remove from heat. Cool down to room temperature. Spread chili mixture on dehydrator tray lined with parchment paper or non-stick sheet. Dehydrate for 8 to 10 hours at 125F till brittle. Pack the dried meal in zipper top plastic bag. Store till ready to use.

Nutrition:

Calories: 250

Fat: 4 grams

Carbs: 44 grams

Protein: 13 grams

135. Spicy Turkey Jerky

Preparation Time: 2 hours

Cooking Time: 6 hours

Servings: 2

Ingredients:

2 pounds turkey breast, boneless and skinless

¾ cup soy sauce

3 tablespoons honey

2 tablespoons chili-garlic paste

2 teaspoons red chili flakes, dried

Directions:

Lay turkey breast flat on a baking sheet. Cover using a plastic wrap. Freeze for 2 hours.

Remove from freezer. Trim fat and membranes. Slice into ¼-inch-thick strips.

Place remaining ingredients in a baking pan. Mix thoroughly.

Add turkey strips to the marinade. Coat thoroughly.

Cover baking pan. Place in the fridge for 12 hours.

Remove from fridge. Drain off excess marinade using a colander.

Place turkey strips on the dehydrator. Leave ½-inch space in between strips.
Dry for 6 hours at 125 F.

Nutrition:

Calories: 574

Fat: 3 grams

Carbs: 33 grams

Protein: 101 grams

136. Cajun Beef Jerky

Preparation Time: 8 hours

Cooking Time: 9 to 10 hours

Servings: 4

Ingredients:

1-pound lean beef, eye of round

2 tablespoons paprika, sweet

4 teaspoons brown sugar, packed

2 teaspoons mustard, dry

2 teaspoons salt

½ teaspoon cayenne pepper

½ teaspoon ginger, ground

¼ teaspoon allspice, ground

Directions:

Place meat in the freezer for 30 minutes.

Cut into ¼-inch thick strips.

Combine all non-meat ingredients in a bowl.

Add meat strips to the marinade. Cover and marinate for 8 hours in the fridge.

Preheat oven to 350 F. Bake meat strips for 10 minutes.

Place meat strips on the dehydrator.

Dry for 9 hours at 155 F.

Nutrition:

Calories: 152

Fat: 4 grams

Carbs: 9 gramsProtein: 21 grams

137. Chicken Pasta Primavera

Preparation Time: 15 minutes

Cooking Time: 8 hours

Servings: 2

Ingredients:

½ cup macaroni noodles

¼ cup dehydrated chicken

2 tablespoons parmesan cheese powder

1 tablespoon powdered milk

½ teaspoon dried basil

½ teaspoon garlic powder

½ teaspoon cornstarch

Salt and pepper to taste

1 ¼ cup water to rehydrate

¼ cup dehydrated vegetables (peas, carrots, onion, bell pepper mix)

Directions:

Cook noodles per package instructions. Drain. Rinse with cold water. Dry overnight at 115 F. Combine powdered ingredients in a small plastic bag, which is your sauce mix. Combine dehydrated noodles, dehydrated chicken and dehydrated vegetables in a large plastic bag. Store the small plastic bag inside the large plastic bag. Add all ingredients, except for the sauce mix, in a pan with the water. Soak for 5 minutes.   Bring to a boil. Cook for 2 minutes. Remove from heat. Add the sauce mix. Let sit for 10 minutes.

Nutrition:

Calories: 182

Fat: 3 grams

Carbs: 27 grams

Protein: 11 grams

138. Beef Taco Mac

Preparation Time: 15 minutes

Cooking Time: 8 hours

Servings: 2

Ingredients:

½ cup macaroni noodles

¼ cup dehydrated ground beef

2 slices dried jalapeno peppers

2 tablespoons powdered cheese

1 tablespoon powdered milk

½ teaspoon dried cilantro

½ teaspoon garlic powder

½ teaspoon taco seasoning

½ teaspoon cornstarch

Salt and pepper to taste

1 ¼ cup water to rehydrate

¼ cup dehydrated vegetables (tomatoes, onions, bell pepper mix, corn)

Directions:

Cook noodles per package instructions. Drain. Rinse with cold water. Dry overnight at 115 F. Combine powdered ingredients in a small plastic bag, which is your sauce mix. Combine dehydrated noodles, dehydrated ground beef and dehydrated vegetables in a large plastic bag. Store the small plastic bag inside the large plastic bag. Add all ingredients, except for the sauce mix, in a pan with the water. Soak for 5 minutes.   Bring to a boil. Cook for 2 minutes. Remove from heat. Add the sauce mix. Let sit for 10 minutes.

Nutrition:

Calories: 23

Fat: 7 grams

Carbs: 29 grams

Protein: 15 grams

139. Curry Rice with Chicken and Cashews

Preparation Time: 10 minutes

Cooking Time: 23 hours

Servings: 2

Ingredients:

2/3 cup instant brown rice

¼ cup chicken, chopped, dried and frozen

¼ cup cashews, roasted and chopped

¼ cup mixed vegetables, dried and frozen

1 ½ teaspoon chicken flavor base, powdered

1 ½ teaspoon curry powder

1 teaspoon chia seeds

1 teaspoon onion flakes, dried

¼ teaspoon garlic powder

¼ teaspoon salt

1/8 teaspoon black pepper, ground

1 ½ cup water

Directions:

Dehydrate each ingredient that needs to be dried separately: chicken and mixed vegetables. Follow required time and temperature for each. Chicken – dry for 12 hours at 125 F Mixed vegetables – dry for 11 hours at 125 F Add all ingredients except the water in a resealable bag. Store until ready to use. Bring water to a boil. Rest the resealable bag on a bowl. Open and pour in boiling water. Seal. Soak for 9 minutes. Turn upside down to mix. Transfer to a bowl.

Nutrition:

Calories: 427

Fat: 12 grams

Carbs: 66 grams

Protein: 15 grams

140. Thai Peanut Noodles with Chicken and Vegetables

Preparation Time: 10 minutes

Cooking Time: 23 hours

Servings: 4

Ingredients:

1 cup pasta

¼ cup chicken, chopped, dried and frozen

¼ cup peanuts, roasted and chopped

¼ cup mixed vegetables, dried and frozen

2 tablespoons peanut butter, powdered

1 ½ teaspoon chicken flavor base, powdered

1 ½ teaspoon cilantro, dried and frozen

1 teaspoon chia seeds

¼ teaspoon garlic powder

¼ teaspoon ginger, ground

¼ teaspoon salt

1/8 teaspoon black pepper, ground

Pinch of cayenne pepper, ground

1 cup water

Directions:

Dehydrate each ingredient that needs to be dried separately: chicken and mixed vegetables. Follow required time and temperature for each. Chicken – dry for 12 hours at 125 F Mixed vegetables – dry for 11 hours at 125 F Add all ingredients except the water in a resealable bag.   Store until ready to use. Bring water to a boil.   Rest the resealable bag on a bowl. Open and pour in boiling water. Seal.   Soak for 9 minutes.   Turn upside down to mix. Transfer to a bowl.

Nutrition:

Calories: 283

Fat: 13 grams

Carbs: 31 grams

Protein: 13 grams

141. Fiesta Rice with Corn and Chicken

Preparation Time: 10 minutes

Cooking Time: 32 hours

Servings: 2

Ingredients:

2/3 cup instant brown rice

1/3 cup chicken, chopped, dried and frozen

½ cup corn, dried and frozen

¼ cup tomatoes, chopped, dried and frozen

1 ½ teaspoon chicken flavor base, powdered

1 ½ teaspoon chili powder

1 teaspoon chia seeds

1 teaspoon onion flakes, dried

½ teaspoon cilantro, dried and frozen

¼ teaspoon cumin

¼ teaspoon garlic powder

¼ teaspoon jalapeno, minced and dried

¼ teaspoon oregano, dried

¼ teaspoon salt

1/8 teaspoon black pepper, ground

1 ½ cup water

Directions:

Dehydrate each ingredient that needs to be dried separately: chicken, corn and tomatoes. Follow required time and temperature for each. Chicken – dry for 12 hours at 125 F Corn – dry for 12 hours at 135 F Tomatoes – dry for 8 hours at 135 F Add all ingredients except the water in a resealable bag. Store until ready to use. Bring water to a boil.   Rest the resealable bag on a bowl. Open and pour in boiling water. Seal. Soak for 9 minutes.   Turn upside down to mix. Transfer to a bowl.

Nutrition:

Calories: 383

Fat: 6 grams

Carbs: 69 grams

Protein: 14 grams

142. Creamy Alfredo Noodles with Chicken, Mushrooms and Pine Nuts

Preparation Time: 10 minutes

Cooking Time: 26 hours

Servings: 4

Ingredients:

1 cup pasta

¼ cup chicken, chopped, dried and frozen

¼ cup pine nuts, toasted

¼ cup mushrooms, chopped, dried and frozen

3 tablespoons Parmesan cheese, grated

2 tablespoons instant dried buttermilk powder

2 tablespoons cornstarch

1 ½ teaspoon chicken flavor base, powdered

1 teaspoon chia seeds

¾ teaspoon dried Italian herb blend

¼ teaspoon garlic powder

¼ teaspoon salt

1/8 teaspoon black pepper, ground

1 ¼ cup water

Directions:

Dehydrate each ingredient that needs to be dried separately: chicken and mushrooms. Follow required time and temperature for each.

Chicken – dry for 12 hours at 125 F

Mushrooms – dry for 14 hours at 130 F

Add all ingredients except the water in a resealable bag.

Bring water to a boil.

Rest the resealable bag on a bowl. Open and pour in boiling water.

Seal. Soak for 9 minutes.

Turn upside down to mix.

Transfer to a bowl.

Nutrition:

Calories: 227

Fat: 8 grams

Carbs: 28 grams

Protein: 11 grams

143. Couscous with Chicken and Vegetables

Preparation Time: 10 minutes

Cooking Time: 23 hours

Servings: 2

Ingredients:

1/3 cup whole wheat couscous

1/3 cup chicken, chopped, dried and frozen

½ cup mixed vegetables, dried and frozen

1 ½ teaspoon chicken flavor base, powdered

1 teaspoon chia seeds

1 teaspoon onion flakes, dried

¼ teaspoon dried parsley

¼ teaspoon dried thyme

¼ teaspoon garlic powder

¼ teaspoon sage

¼ teaspoon salt

1/8 teaspoon black pepper, ground

1 ½ cup water

Directions:

Dehydrate each ingredient that needs to be dried separately: chicken and mixed vegetables. Follow required time and temperature for each.

Chicken – dry for 12 hours at 125 F

Mixed vegetables – dry for 11 hours at 125 F

Add all ingredients except the water in a resealable bag.

Store until ready to use.

Bring water to a boil.

Rest the resealable bag on a bowl. Open and pour in boiling water.

Seal. Soak for 9 minutes.

Turn upside down to mix.

Transfer to a bowl.

Nutrition:

Calories: 156

Fat: 2 grams

Carbs: 25 grams

Protein: 10 grams

144. Root Bark Stew

Preparation Time: 15 minutes

Cooking Time: 20 hours

Servings: 4

Ingredients:

1 large sweet potato

1-pound parsnips

1 large rutabaga

3 medium turnips

2 medium onions, chopped

2 cloves garlic, minced

16 ounces chicken broth

1 can diced tomatoes, drained

¼ cup raisins

1 tablespoon curry powder

1 tablespoon ground cumin

1 tablespoon olive oil

1 teaspoon cinnamon

Salt and pepper to taste

Directions:

Peel and dice roots into ½-inch cubes.

Sauté onion for 5 minutes in non-stick pan over medium-high heat.

Add garlic, curry, cumin, cinnamon and a splash of chicken broth. Stir for another minute.

In a large pot, put the contents of the pan. Add diced roots and raisins. Add enough chicken broth to cover roots.

Bring to a boil. Reduce heat. Cover and simmer for 10 minutes. Stir occasionally.

Add diced tomatoes, salt and pepper. Simmer for 5 more minutes. Drain off broth into pot.

To make the bark - Put broth and 4 cups of cooked roots into a blender. Blend until smooth.

Spread ¼-inch thick mixture on the dehydrator tray lined with drying sheet. Dry for 8 hours at 135 F.

Put remaining cooked roots on the dehydrator tray. Dry for 12 hours at 135 F.

Let cool before packing. Combine roots and bark into individual meal servings and pack in plastic bags.

Combine ¾ cup dried root pieces, ¼ cup dried root bark and 1 cup water. Soak for 5 minutes.

Bring to a boil. Cook for 1 minute.

Nutrition:

Calories: 301

Fat: 5 grams

Carbs: 62 grams

Protein: 7 grams

145. Black Beans and Rice

Preparation Time: 20 minutes

Cooking Time: 6 hours

Servings: 4

Ingredients:

1 cup white rice, cooked

1/2 cup chicken breast, cubed

1/2 cup black beans, steamed

1/4 cup green bell pepper, chopped

2 tablespoons cilantro

1/2 teaspoon garlic powder

1 tablespoon vegetable oil

Directions:

In a small skillet, heat oil over medium heat and add the chicken. Cook until cooked through and remove from heat. In a large bowl, combine the chicken, rice, beans, bell pepper, cilantro, and garlic powder. Mix well. Place ParaFlexx Screens on the racks of your Excalibur Food Dehydrator and spread the mixture evenly on the screens. Set your Excalibur to 125F and dehydrate for 6 hours. Store mixture in zipper lock bags until ready to use. To rehydrate, combine the contents of the bag with 1 1/4 cup boiling water and stir well. Cover and let stand 10 minutes before serving.

Nutrition:

Calories: 317

Fat: 4.8 g grams

Carbs: 52.9 grams

Protein: 14.6 grams

146. White Bean Dip with Tomatoes

Preparation Time: 5 minutes

Cooking Time: 15 minutes

Servings: 4

Ingredients:

1 can cannellini beans; soaked overnight

1 small white onion; peeled and diced

6 sun-dried tomatoes

3 tablespoons chopped parsley

1½ teaspoon minced garlic; divided

1¼ cups water

1 teaspoon paprika

3 tablespoons olive oil

2 tablespoons lemon juice

1 tablespoon capers

1 teaspoon salt

1/8 teaspoon ground black pepper

Directions:

Drain beans and place in the Foodi. Pour in water and add 1 teaspoon garlic, salt, and black pepper.

Plug in and switch on the Foodi and secure with lid. Then position pressure indicator, select Pressure and cook at HIGH pressure for 14 minutes

When the timer beeps, switch off the Foodi and let pressure release naturally for 10 minutes and then do quick pressure release.

In the meantime, place a small non-stick frying pan over medium heat, add oil and let heat.

Then add onion and remaining garlic and cook for 3 to 5 minutes or until onions are nicely golden brown.

When the onions are done, set pan aside until required. Then uncover the pot and drain beans, reserve 1/2 cup of cooking liquid

Let beans cool slightly and then transfer to a food processor and add onion-garlic mixture, paprika, and lemon juice.

Pulse until smooth; slowly blend in reserved cooking liquid until dip reaches to desired thickness. Tip mixture into a serving bowl

Dice tomatoes and stir together with capers and parsley

Add this mixture into bean dip and stir until mixed well. Adjust the seasoning and serve immediately.

Nutrition:

Calories: 128

Fat: 11 grams

Carbs: 8 grams

Protein: 1.9 grams

147. Black bean and corn salad

Preparation Time: 10 minutes

Cooking Time: 24 Minutes

Servings: 4

Ingredients:

2 cups dried black beans

1 medium fresh jalapeño chili; stemmed and split lengthwise

2 cups fresh corn kernels-about 2 large ears), or frozen kernels, thawed

1 large globe or beefsteak tomato; chopped

6 medium scallions; thinly sliced

1 medium yellow bell pepper, stemmed, cored, and diced

5 tablespoons olive oil

2 teaspoon cumin seeds

2 teaspoon minced garlic

1/4 cup fresh lime juice

1 tablespoon sherry vinegar

1 tablespoon honey

1 teaspoon salt

Directions:

Soak the beans in a large bowl of water on the counter overnight, for at least 12 hours or up to 16 hours. Drain them in a colander set in the sink

Heat the oil in the Foodi turned to the *Sautéing/Browning* function. Add the cumin seeds and garlic; cook for 1 minute, stirring constantly, just until the garlic begins to brown. Pour in the drained beans; add the jalapeño. Add enough cool tap water so that the ingredients are submerged by 2 inches-the seeds will float).

Lock the lid on the Foodi and then cook On High pressure for 18 minutes. To get 18 minutes' cook time, press Pressure button and use the time adjustment button to adjust the cook time to18 minutes.

Pressure release use the Quick Pressure Release method

Unlock and open the cooker. Drain the contents of the cooker into a colander set in the sink. Discard the jalapeño

Transfer the bean mixture to a large bowl; stir in the corn, tomato, scallions, and bell pepper. Whisk the lime juice, olive oil, vinegar, honey, and salt in a small bowl until smooth; pour over the salad and toss well.

Nutrition:

Calories: 423

Fat: 8.7 grams

Carbs: 68.2 grams

Protein: 21.6 grams

148. Wild Rice with Sweet Potatoes

Preparation Time: 15 minutes

Cooking Time: 50 Minutes

Servings: 6

Ingredients:

1 medium yellow onion, chopped

2 medium celery stalks; chopped

1½ cups black wild rice-about 8 oz.)

3 cups vegetable or chicken broth

1 large sweet potato-about 1 lb.); peeled and diced

1/4 cup dried cranberries

2 tablespoons olive oil

1 tablespoon packed fresh sage leaves; minced

2 teaspoon fresh thyme leaves

1/2 teaspoon salt

1/2 teaspoon ground black pepper

Directions:

Heat the olive oil in the Foodi turned to the *Sautéing/Browning* function. Add the onion and celery; cook, stirring often, until the onion softens, about 4 minutes. Mix in the sage and thyme; cook until fragrant, about 30 seconds. Stir in the rice and toss well to coat. Pour in the broth; stir well to get up any browned bits in the bottom of pot.

Lock the lid on the Foodi and then cook On High pressure for 30 minutes. To get 30 minutes' cook time, press Pressure button

Pressure Release Use the Quick Pressure Release method to return the pot's pressure to normal.

Unlock and open the cooker. Stir in the sweet potato, cranberries, salt, and pepper.

Lock the lid back on the Foodi and then cook On High pressure for 15 minutes. To get 15 minutes' cook time, press Pressure button

Pressure Release Use the Quick Pressure Release method to return the pot's pressure to normal. Unlock and open the cooker. Stir well before serving.

Nutrition:

Calories: 106

Fat: 8.1 grams

Carbs: 4.4 grams

Protein: 4 grams

149. Seedylicious Granola

Preparation Time: 35 minutes

Cooking Time: 4 to 6 hours

Servings: 3

Ingredients:

1/2 cup pumpkin seeds

1/4 cup shelled sunflower seeds

1/2 cup flaxseed

1/2 cup chia seeds

1 teaspoon ground cinnamon

1/2 teaspoon salt

Some ground cloves or 1/8 teaspoon

2 tablespoon honey

1 egg white, beaten until fluffy

Directions:

Spread the non-stick fruit-leather sheets on the dehydrator trays.

Heat a dry skillet on medium-high heat. Then, warm the pumpkin seeds while keep stirring.

When the seeds start to pop and snap vigorously after 2 to 4 minutes, pour onto a baking sheet. It will take approximately 2 to 4 minutes.

Similarly, heat the sunflower seeds in the same way. When the seeds change color somewhat and start to pop after 1 minute or so, pour onto the baking sheet.

Repeat the same process with flax seeds and chia seeds. Chia seeds will not pop as much as other seeds. Let all the seeds cool completely.

Add all seeds into a large bowl, then add the cinnamon, salt, and cloves.

Mix the honey briskly into the egg white and pour into the seed mixture.

Blend well with a wooden spoon to evenly dispense the egg mixture thoroughly into the seeds.

Pour the seed mixture onto the prepared trays. Press it into a very thin and even layer.

Dehydrate at 160° to 165°F for about 4 to 6 hours, or until the granola is dry to the touch on the top and bottom surfaces and crunchy.

Let cool completely. Break into small chunks and store in an airtight container in a cool dark place for up to 2 weeks.

Nutrition:

Calories: 130

Fat: 8 grams

Carbs: 11 grams

Protein: 5 grams

150. Coconut Berry Muesli

Preparation Time: 1 hour

Cooking Time: 2 to 4 hours

Servings: 4

Ingredients:

½ cup dried strawberries or 2 cups of fresh strawberries, stemmed and cut into 1/8-inch slices

1 1/2 cups rye flakes

1 1/2 cup rolled oats (not quick-cooking)

2 tablespoon agave syrup

2 tablespoon coconut oil, melted

3/4 teaspoon fine sea salt

1/2 cup almonds

1/2 cup unsweetened coconut flakes/chips

Directions:

If using fresh strawberries, dehydrate by spreading them on dehydrator trays lined with lightly greased non-stick mesh sheets. Preferred temperature and drying time is 135°F and 8 to 12 hours, or until completely dry and crisp. Let them cool completely. If using dried strawberries, skip this step.

Preheat the oven to 325°F.

Mix the rye flakes and oats with salt, agave syrup, and coconut oil, in a large mixing bowl.

To ensure even distribution toss all the ingredients well.

Then, spread out the mixture in a thin layer on a rimmed baking sheet.

Bake for 15 minutes, or until the rye and oats, are lightly toasted. Let them cool completely.

Spread out the almonds on a baking sheet and toast in the oven until the nuts are warm and slightly browned from the mid, or for 12 to 14 minutes. Let them cool completely, and then chop roughly.

Put the coconut flakes on a baking sheet. Roast them in the oven for 8 to 10 minutes, or until the coconut is slightly browned from the edges. Let cool.

In a large bowl, mix the rye-oatmeal mixture, chopped almonds, toasted coconut, and the dried strawberries. Muesli is ready to use. Safe in an airtight jar or container in a cool dark place for up to 2 weeks.

Nutrition:

Calories: 205

Fat: 7 grams

Carbs: 26 grams

Protein: 6 grams

Conclusion

Food drying is one of the oldest known methods of preserving food. Way back before there were grocery stores in every town and refrigerators in every almost every home in the Western world, people had to come up with ways to make the harvest last into the winter months.

Our not-so-distant ancestors didn't have the convenience of grocery stores packed full of food imported in from all over the world. If they wanted something, they had to grow it, buy it or trade for it, and they were largely at the mercy of Mother Nature. Fruits and vegetables weren't available year-round like they are now, so if people wanted to eat healthy food during the winter, they had to figure out ways to preserve the harvest to make it last year-round.

Back then, learning to dry and otherwise preserve food was something people had to know in order to survive, especially in places with harsh winter climates where it was impossible to grow produce during the winter. Once the first frost set in, the ground would soon freeze solid. Intense cold and heavy snow made working the fields impossible. Having food put away for the winter literally meant the difference between going to bed with a full stomach and slowly starving to death.

Now, take some time out to sit down and think about preserving and storing food through dehydration, and have a particle understanding of steps, tools, and techniques required for it. It will prove to be a significant change in your kitchen habits and lifestyles.

I believe that once you get a handle on the basic techniques, you can start growing and branching out into all kinds of other creative and novel endeavors of dehydrating foods. Just keep it simple at the start for the sake of gaining enough experience. Once you become a grand maestro of dehydration and you've got a bunch of successful batches put up for the season, then you can start playing with your creative ideas.

Remember, different foods have different timings and pre-treatments, so you must follow each step accordingly. Thoroughly drying the food is the key to successful dehydration. The presence of liquid in the dehydrated food turn it fetid and prone to many harmful bacteria such as E. coli. Also, selecting the best quality food ensures a healthy and perfect dried food. Always prefer farmer's market for selecting fruits and vegetables as they provide the freshest food.

When you start to head off with your creative ideas for dehydration, try to limit it to one or two new ingredients. Occasionally what appears to be a great idea, can muddle the flavors or emphasize the taste of the original fruit, vegetable or meat. Limiting the ingredients to one or two possible suspects will enable you to distinguish the culprit quickly.

Storing dried food is a crucial step to ensure the most extended shelf life. If not stored well, moisture, heat and oxygen decrease the shelf life and turn them bad sooner than expected. Store you dehydrated bounties in a cool and dry place, or in zip lock bags in the freezer to ensure longer shelf life. You can increase it by vacuum sealing the bags and then store them in the freezer.

Before you get too enthusiastic about dehydrating batches upon batches of dried foods and pilling your pantry up with all your favorite foods, you need to look and practice all the rules of dehydration and have an idea for the space you have for storing; it will be of no use if you are drying more than the available space unless you intend to sell or gift them. Finally, I wish you a happy dehydrating journey. Enjoy the process of drying your bounty and remember to follow safe practices while drying your food.

I want you, the reader, to know that your review is very important and so if you'd like to leave a review, all you have to do is click here. I wish you all the best in your future success!

Let's promote organic food preservation.

Wish you success!